A Child's Garden
of Verses

PRESENTED TO

WITH LOVE, FROM

DATE

Published in Nashville, Tennessee, by Tommy Nelson™, a division of Thomas Nelson, Inc.
Vice President of Children's Books: Laura Minchew
Project Manager: Karen Gallini; Editor: Tama Fortner

Designed by Koechel Peterson & Associates

Library of Congress Cataloging-in-Publication Data

A child's garden of verses / with the artwork of Thomas Kinkade ; a collection of scriptures,
prayers & poems, featuring the works of Robert Louis Stevenson ; compiled by June Ford.
     p.   cm.
    Includes indexes.
    Summary: A collection of poems by Robert Louis Stevenson and others which reflect
the joys of childhood, accompanied by Bible verses.
    ISBN 0-8499-5869-5
    1. Children's poetry, English. 2. Christian poetry, English. 3. Children's poetry,
American. 4. Christian poetry, American. [1. Poetry Collections.] I. Stevenson, Robert
Louis, 1850–1894. II. Kinkade, Thomas, 1958– ill. III. Ford, June, 1957–
PR1175.3.C467   1999   99-20086
                                                       CIP

Printed in the United States of America

99 00 01 02 03 04 RRD 9 8 7 6 5 4 3 2 1

A Child's Garden of Verses

A Collection of Scriptures, Prayers, & Poems
Featuring the Works of
ROBERT LOUIS STEVENSON

With the artwork of
THOMAS KINKADE

Compiled by June Ford

Tommy NELSON

Thomas Nelson, Inc.
Nashville

TO ANY READER

As from the house your mother sees
You playing round the garden trees,
So you may see, if you will look
Through the windows of this book,
Another child, far, far away,
And in another garden, play.

But do not think you can at all,
By knocking on the window, call
That child to hear you. He intent
Is all on his play-business bent.

He does not hear; he will not look,
Nor yet be lured out of this book.
For, long ago, the truth to say,
He has grown up and gone away,
And it is but a child of air
That lingers in the garden there.

ROBERT LOUIS STEVENSON

A book is like a garden

carried in a pocket.

CHINESE PROVERB

CONTENTS

ABOUT THOMAS KINKADE
Painter of Light™

AN EARLY START

Thomas Kinkade began his painting career early in life—very early. Though he was only four years old, Kinkade remembers clearly the day that his older sister showed him a picture she had drawn of a house with some parallel lines next to it representing a road. He took the drawing from her and said, "No, let me show you." Kinkade erased her road and redrew the lines so that they grew closer together as they neared the edge of the paper, and his sister said, "Oh, that looks better!" It was then that Kinkade realized he could draw the world in three dimensions, in a way that was believable to people.

From that point on, painting was Kinkade's passion. He chose not to watch television, so that he could paint. He chose not to play on his school's sports teams, so that he could paint. Every spare minute was spent painting, sketching, and trying out new art techniques and materials. His first studio was a crowded laundry room where he worked at a makeshift easel that he had built himself from an old desk and some plywood. A paper route and other odd jobs provided him with money for supplies. And Kinkade felt very blessed.

"All I wanted to do was sketch and draw. I knew even then that if I couldn't make a good living at it, I would still have to pursue my love of my hobby, my passion, which was being able to use paints to create a beautiful new world."

THE IMPORTANCE OF FAMILY

Family has always been important to Thomas Kinkade. Growing up, Kinkade and his siblings were the only children in their small town school whose parents were divorced. That fact had a big impact on Kinkade, but in a surprisingly positive way.

"People tend to think of divorce as a negative experience. But in my case," explains Kinkade, *"it really fueled a sense that family was the utter foundation for this life. No matter what else I did with my life, I knew I wanted to be a husband and a dad."*

Today, Kinkade and his wife, Nanette, have four wonderful daughters—Merritt, Chandler, Winsor, and Everett. Each girl is named after an artist whose works the Kinkades admire. Merritt is named after William Merritt Chase (1849–1916), an American painter; Chandler after Howard Chandler Christy (1873–1952), an American illustrator and painter; Winsor after Winsor McCay (d. 1934), an American cartoonist and pioneer of cartoon films; and Everett after John Everett Millais (1829–1896), an English painter. More importantly, each girl has the middle name of "Christian," because the Kinkades see Christ as the center of each girl's life.

A READING RITUAL

Prior to the birth of their daughters, Kinkade and his wife decided that they wanted to savor every moment with their children.

"Our biggest hobby is spending time together as a family, and that can be defined in some of the simplest ways," says Kinkade.

One of those ways is the family's favorite evening ritual—reading.

"We are a book family. We don't even have a television in our home. Nanette and I wanted to teach the love of reading by example. So, when our girls were very young, we began reading to each of them every night. Our favorite books are ones that involve lots of imagination."

When the Kinkade children are old enough to read, they are allowed to read in the family room with their mother and father.

"We all have our own special chair with a light next to it," Kinkade says. "It's a peaceful, comfortable setting in our family room, when the lights go on in the quiet of the evening. Undisturbed. We all sit and read."

A FAMILY OF FAITH

The foundation of the Kinkade family is its faith in God. Each evening, the Kinkades have chapel with their children.

"We are a family of prayer," declares Kinkade. "I believe that the kids like the worship time. We read a Bible story, talk about it, and then pray. It only takes about ten minutes, but it lays a steady foundation for the family."

Kinkade's devotion to family and to God is evident in his life and in his work. Of his personal and professional successes, Kinkade acknowledges:

"I am very humbly aware that this has been God's doing from day one. I'm really just a small-town kid. I've just been given a chance to use my talents in ways God chooses—and it is certainly his doing, not mine."

Let your light so shine before men,
that they may see your good works and glorify your Father in heaven.

MATTHEW 5:16 NKJV

*"The paintings I create are really nothing more
or less than an outgrowth of my desire
to share God's love and grace with others."*

THOMAS KINKADE

IT'S ALL IN THE DETAILS

Did you know that Thomas Kinkade often hides his family's initials and names in his paintings? Sometimes, Kinkade paints himself, his family, and even the family pets into his works!

"When my career began to blossom and I published our first print," says Kinkade, *"I wanted to offer a tribute to my wife, Nanette. So, I put an N on the side of a little boat that was in the painting."*

Since then, Kinkade has hidden little *N's* in the sky, on the side of a barn, under the wing of a bird, and in countless other places. As each of their daughters was born, Kinkade also began putting their initials, names, and images in some of his paintings.

"I even did a series of paintings featuring little cottages that were named after my daughters. It's my way of saying that my family is my priority."

As you look through the pages of this book, try to find Kinkade's hidden details. Here are some clues to get you started. Look for the letter N in the sign above. In *Paris, Eiffel Tower,* below,

can you tell who is painting at the edge of the Seine River? That's Thomas Kinkade himself!

Some of Kinkade's paintings, such as *Paris, City of Lights,* have even more details to offer. Look closely, and you will find Kinkade painting the sights of Paris as his oldest daughter, Merritt, looks on. Kinkade even signed his painting

within a painting—the smallest Kinkade signature on record! Behind them is the Café Nanette, named after his beloved wife. And in front of the café is the real Nanette holding baby Chandler as she hails a cab. In all, fifteen hidden *N's* can be found in this painting as a further tribute to Nanette.

LEARNING ABOUT YOUR OWN SPECIAL TALENT

God uses many tools in this world to expand his kingdom and to touch people. For Thomas Kinkade, God uses painting. *You* also have a talent that can be used to glorify God. The key is to find and develop that talent.

"When you read the Gospel, you start to see God's embracing love through his created world. When I paint the world," says Kinkade, "I am really painting God's love for us."

If you believe that your talent lies in painting or drawing or any other area, Kinkade advises you to first let it become your hobby.

"Let it be something that you get so excited about doing that you will say no to other things to do this. It becomes a joy that is as much fun as anything you can possibly do. Let the Lord give you that delight—so that as you work, it becomes more than just an interest, it becomes a passion."

To develop your talent, take time to work on it each day. Learn to enjoy your small successes, because they will add up to larger ones.

"The great thing about art is that you can look at a painting and immediately compare it to the painting right next to it, and see the results of those little successes you have had. The little successes become the things that fuel you to keep going."

If you do want to learn to draw, Kinkade advises that all you really need is a pencil, some paper, your imagination, and the desire to go out and explore life. It can also be helpful to have your own space in which to work. Ask your parents if you might set up a little studio somewhere. It can be just a corner of the garage or any other unused space. Most importantly, be open to God's inspiration. In Kinkade's case, there is no part of the creative process that he doesn't consider to be in some way divinely inspired.

"Throughout the day God is painting little visions in my heart and giving me ideas," says Kinkade. "Many times when I am at the end of any ideas I might have on my own, God will graciously drop an idea into my midst that seems to come out of nowhere. My part is very easy. All I have to do is have my radar up and my sketchpad always at the ready."

"I firmly believe that every child is born as a package of talents, abilities, expectations, and enthusiasm. If we really commit our talents to the Lord—be it a talent in painting, or in business, communications, writing, math, or whatever the talent is in—I believe God can use that talent to bless others."

Imagine that the year is 1850, and you have been born into a world where there are no computers, no television sets, no movies, and no telephones. Houses do not have electricity. Cars and airplanes are just the wild dreams of crazy inventors. Travel is slow and must be done by ship, train, wagon, horse, or foot. To write, you must use a pen that is dipped in ink from a glass jar. And the paper you use is handmade. Now, consider writing this book out word-for-word by hand—and being sick while you do it. That is what life was like for Robert Louis Stevenson, Scottish poet, essayist, short-story writer, and novelist.

Stevenson, author of some of the world's best-loved poems and novels including *Treasure Island, New Arabian Nights, Dr. Jekyll and Mr. Hyde,* and *Kidnapped*, was born in Edinburgh, Scotland. He was the only son of Thomas Stevenson, a lighthouse engineer, and his wife, Maggie. Stevenson was a sickly infant and suffered from terrible breathing problems. When he was eighteen months old, the Stevensons hired a nurse, Alison Cunningham. Alison served as the young boy's nanny and lived in the house with the family. She soon became as devoted to the child as his own loving parents.

As a child, Stevenson began calling his nurse Cummy. Since his health had not greatly improved, and he was not allowed out in the winter, Cummy became his friend, confidante, and companion. He and Cummy would sit at the window and watch as the other children played and the grown-ups went about their work. Often, Cummy would read him stories. And, as young as the age of four, Stevenson began writing stories and poems of his own for Cummy.

Although Stevenson remained in frail health, he eventually attended school and became a lawyer, though he never practiced law. His true love, he said, was writing.

Stevenson wrote in *The Art of Writing*:

Sooner or later, somehow, anyhow, I was bound to write a novel. It seems vain to ask why. Men are born with various manias: from my earliest childhood, it was mine to make a plaything of imaginary series of events; and as soon as I was able to write, I became a good friend to the paper-makers.

As a young man, Stevenson began traveling around the world, both to see its wonders and to search for a cure for his illness. Already a prolific writer, Stevenson wrote about his travels in his many short stories, poems, and novels. Unfortunately, however, Stevenson's travels did not lead to a cure for his condition. Rather, it is believed that he contracted tuberculosis during either one of his sea voyages or while traveling on an emigrant train. Stevenson's condition worsened, yet he continued to travel and write.

In 1880, Stevenson married Fanny Osbourne and became the stepfather of her son, Lloyd, and daughter, Isobel.

Stevenson often amused Lloyd with poems and stories that he created from his memories of childhood and his time with Cummy. At one point, when Stevenson was too weak even to hold a pen, Lloyd—who was then only about ten years old—diligently took notes on all of Stevenson's wonderful memories. The result was *A Child's Garden of Verses*, in which Stevenson immortalized Cummy and many of his family members in poetry.

In 1890, due to Stevenson's poor health, the family moved to Vailima in Samoa, where his widowed mother soon joined them. The Samoans adored Stevenson and he them. They named him "Tusitala," which means "the storyteller." Stevenson died there from a stroke in 1894 and was buried on the summit of Mount Vaea.

Stevenson's works, however, have lived on, easily withstanding the test of time. They continue to be reprinted in various forms and several have even been made into successful movies.

A Time to Play

Children are a gift from the Lord.

PSALM 127:3

MARCHING SONG

Bring the comb and play upon it!
    Marching, here we come!
Willie cocks his highland bonnet,
    Johnnie beats the drum.

Mary Jane commands the party,
    Peter leads the rear;
Fleet in time, alert and hearty,
    Each a Grenadier!

All in the most martial manner
    Marching double-quick;
While the napkin like a banner
    Waves upon the stick!

Here's enough of fame and pillage,
    Great commander Jane!
Now that we've been round the village,
    Let's go home again.

ROBERT LOUIS STEVENSON

THE SINGING CHILDREN

Gladly marching two and two,
Keeping time as soldiers do,
Waving banner, beating drum,
Here the singing children come!
Clean and happy, good and neat,
What a sight for all the street!
Smiling mothers, come and see,
Here's an army brave and free
Whose unlessoned fearless feet
Need not yet to learn retreat:
Waving banner, beating drum,
Here the singing children come!

MAUDE KEARY

God has put something noble and good
into every heart his hand created.

MARK TWAIN

COME, MY CHILDREN

Come, my children, come away,
For the sun shines bright today;
Little children, come with me,
Birds and brooks and posies see;
Get your hats and come away,
For it is a pleasant day.

Everything is laughing, singing,
All the pretty flowers are springing;
See the kitten, full of fun,
Sporting in the brilliant sun;
Children too may sport and play,
For it is a pleasant day.

Bring the hoop, and bring the ball,
Come with happy faces all;
Let us make a merry ring,
Talk and laugh, and dance and sing.
Quickly, quickly, come away,
For it is a pleasant day.

MOTHER GOOSE

SEE HOW THE CHILDREN IN THE PRINT

See how the children in the print
Bound on the book to see what's in 't!
O, like these pretty babes, may you
Seize and *apply* this volume too!
And while your eye upon the cuts
With harmless ardor opes and shuts,
Reader, may your immortal mind
To their sage lessons not be blind.

ROBERT LOUIS STEVENSON

A GOOD PLAY

We built a ship upon the stairs
All made of the back-bedroom chairs,
And filled it full of sofa pillows
To go a-sailing on the billows.

We took a saw and several nails,
And water in the nursery pails;
And Tom said, "Let us also take
An apple and a slice of cake";—
Which was enough for Tom and me
To go a-sailing on, till tea.

We sailed along for days and days,
And had the very best of plays;
But Tom fell out and hurt his knee,
So there was no one left but me.

ROBERT LOUIS STEVENSON

SAILING, SAILING

Sailing, sailing, over the bounding main.

For many a stormy wind shall blow

E'er Jack comes home again.

Oh, sailing, sailing, over the bounding main.

For many a stormy wind shall blow

E'er Jack comes home again.

MOTHER GOOSE

The sea is his because he made it.

PSALM 95:5

THE COW

The friendly cow all red and white,
        I love with all my heart:
She gives me cream with all her might,
        To eat with apple tart.

She wanders lowing here and there,
        And yet she cannot stray,
All in the pleasant open air,
        The pleasant light of day;

And blown by all the winds that pass
        And wet with all the showers,
She walks among the meadow grass
        And eats the meadow flowers.

ROBERT LOUIS STEVENSON

HEY, DIDDLE, DIDDLE!

Hey, diddle, diddle!
        The cat and the fiddle,
The cow jumped over the moon;
        The little dog laughed
        To see such sport,
And the dish ran away with the spoon.

MOTHER GOOSE

ALL THINGS
BRIGHT AND BEAUTIFUL

All things bright and beautiful,
All creatures great and small,
All things wise and wonderful,
The Lord God made them all.

Each little flower that opens,
Each little bird that sings,
He made their glowing colors,
He made their tiny wings.

The purple-headed mountain,
The river running by,
The sunset and the morning
That brightens up the sky,

The cold wind in the winter,
The pleasant summer sun,
The ripe fruits in the garden,
He made them every one.

He gave us eyes to see them,
And lips that we might tell
How great is God Almighty,
Who has made all things well.

CECIL FRANCES ALEXANDER

WHAT IS PINK?

What is pink? a rose is pink
By the fountain's brink.
What is red? a poppy's red
In its barley bed.
What is blue? the sky is blue
Where the clouds float thro'.
What is white? a swan is white
Sailing in the light.
What is yellow? pears are yellow,
Rich and ripe and mellow.
What is green? the grass is green,
With small flowers between.
What is violet? clouds are violet
In the summer twilight.
What is orange? why, an orange,
Just an orange!

CHRISTINA ROSSETTI

THE VIOLET

A violet by a mossy stone,
Half hidden from the eye,
Fair as a star, when only one
Is shining in the sky.

WILLIAM WORDSWORTH

DAISIES

Where innocent bright-eyed daisies are,
With blades of grass between,
Each daisy stands up like a star
Out of a sky of green.

CHRISTINA ROSSETTI

BUTTERFLY, BUTTERFLY

Butterfly, butterfly, whence do you come?
I know not, I ask not, I never had home.
Butterfly, butterfly, where do you go?
Where the sun shines, and where the buds grow.

MOTHER GOOSE

But I tell you that even Solomon with his riches
was not dressed as beautifully as one of these flowers.

MATTHEW 6:29

LITTLE SNAIL

I saw a little snail
Come down the garden walk.
He wagged his head this way . . . that way . . .
Like a clown in a circus.
He looked from side to side
As though he were from a different country.
I have always said he carries his house on his back . . .
Today in the rain
I saw that it was his umbrella!

HILDA CONKLING

Pussy has a whiskered face,
Kitty has such pretty ways;
Doggie scampers when I call,
And has a heart to love us all.

CHRISTINA ROSSETTI

When the cows come home the milk is coming,
Honey's made while the bees are humming;
Duck and drake on the rushy lake,
And the deer live safe in the breezy brake;
And timid, funny, brisk little bunny
Winks his nose and sits all sunny.

CHRISTINA ROSSETTI

Bow, wow, wow!
Whose dog art thou?
Little Tommy Tinker's dog.
Bow, wow, wow!

MOTHER GOOSE

*Then God said, "Let the earth
be filled with animals."*
GENESIS 1:24

MY SHADOW

I have a little shadow that goes in and out with me,
And what can be the use of him is more than I can see.
He is very, very like me from the heels up to the head;
And I see him jump before me, when I jump into my bed.

The funniest thing about him is the way he likes to grow—
Not at all like proper children, which is always very slow;
For he sometimes shoots up taller, like an india-rubber ball,
And he sometimes gets so little that there's none of him at all.

He hasn't got a notion of how children ought to play,
And can only make a fool of me in every sort of way.
He stays so close beside me, he's a coward you can see;
I'd think shame to stick to nursie as that shadow sticks to me!

One morning, very early, before the sun was up,
I rose and found the shining dew on every buttercup;
But my lazy little shadow, like an arrant sleepyhead,
Had stayed at home behind me and was fast asleep in bed.

ROBERT LOUIS STEVENSON

I love you well, my little brother,

And you are fond of me;

Let us be kind to one another,

As brothers ought to be.

You shall learn to play with me,

And learn to use my toys;

And then I think that we shall be

Two happy little boys.

MOTHER GOOSE

Every good action and every perfect gift is from God.

These good gifts come down from the Creator of the sun, moon, and stars.

God does not change like their shifting shadows.

JAMES 1:17

THE LITTLE JUMPING GIRLS

Jump—jump—jump—
    Jump away
From this town into
    The next, today.

Jump—jump—jump—
    Jump over the moon;
Jump all the morning,
    And all the noon.

Jump—jump—jump—
    Jump all night;
Won't our mothers
    Be in a fright?

Jump—jump—jump—
    Over the sea;
What wonderful wonders
    We shall see.

Jump—jump—jump—
    And leave behind
Everything evil
    That we may find.

Jump—jump—jump—
    Jump far away;
And all come home
    Some other day.

KATE GREENAWAY

Jack be nimble,
Jack be quick,
Jack jump over
The candlestick.

Jump it lively,
Jump it quick,
But don't knock over
The candlestick.

MOTHER GOOSE

I want your joy to be the fullest joy.
JOHN 15:11

PICTURE BOOKS IN WINTER

Summer fading, winter comes—
Frosty mornings, tingling thumbs,
Window robins, winter rooks,
And the picture storybooks.

Water now is turned to stone
Nurse and I can walk upon;
Still we find the flowing brooks
In the picture storybooks.

All the pretty things put by,
Wait upon the children's eye,
Sheep and shepherds, trees and crooks
In the picture storybooks.

We may see how all things are,
Seas and cities, near and far,
And the flying fairies' looks,
In the picture storybooks.

How am I to sing your praise,
Happy chimney-corner days,
Sitting safe in nursery nooks,
Reading picture storybooks?

ROBERT LOUIS STEVENSON

WINTERTIME

Late lies the wintry sun a-bed,

A frosty, fiery sleepyhead;

Blinks but an hour or two; and then,

A blood-red orange, sets again.

Before the stars have left the skies,

At morning in the dark I rise;

And shivering in my nakedness,

By the cold candle, bathe and dress.

Close by the jolly fire I sit

To warm my frozen bones a bit;

Or, with a reindeer-sled, explore

The colder countries round the door.

When to go out, my nurse doth wrap

Me in my comforter and cap:

The cold wind burns my face, and blows

Its frosty pepper up my nose.

Black are my steps on silver sod;

Thick blows my frosty breath abroad;

And tree and house, and hill and lake,

Are frosted like a wedding cake.

ROBERT LOUIS STEVENSON

Take away my sin, and I will be clean.
Wash me, and I will be whiter than snow.
PSALM 51:7

THE HAYLOFT

Through all the pleasant meadow-side
        The grass grew shoulder-high,
Till the shining scythes went far and wide
        And cut it down to dry.

These green and sweetly smelling crops
        They led in wagons home;
And they piled them here in mountaintops
        For mountaineers to roam.

Here is Mount Clear, Mount Rusty Nail,
        Mount Eagle and Mount High;—
The mice that in these mountains dwell,
        No happier are than I!

O what a joy to clamber there,
        O what a place for play,
With the sweet, the dim, the dusty air,
        The happy hills of hay.

ROBERT LOUIS STEVENSON

HYMNS IN PROSE FOR CHILDREN

Come, let us go into the thick shade, for it is the noon of day,
and the summer sun beats hot upon our heads.
The shade is pleasant, and cool; the branches meet above our heads,
and shut out the sun, as with a green curtain; the grass is soft to our feet, and
a clear brook washes the roots of the trees. . . .

The cattle can lie down to sleep in the cool shade,
but we can do what is better; we can raise our voices to heaven;
we can praise the great God who made us. He made the warm sun,
and the cool shade; the trees that grow upward, and the brooks that
run murmuring along. All the things that we see are his work.

Can we raise our voices up to the high heaven? can we make him
hear who is above the stars? We need not raise our voices to the stars,
for he heareth us when we only whisper; when we breathe out
words softly with a low voice. He that filleth the heavens is here also.

ANNA LÆTITIA BARBAULD

37

THE UNSEEN PLAYMATE

When children are playing alone on the green,
In comes the playmate that never was seen.
When children are happy and lonely and good,
The Friend of the Children comes out of the wood.

Nobody heard him and nobody saw,
His is a picture you never could draw,
But he's sure to be present, abroad or at home,
When children are happy and playing alone.

He lies in the laurels, he runs on the grass,
He sings when you tinkle the musical glass;
Whene'er you are happy and cannot tell why
The Friend of the Children is sure to be by!

He loves to be little, he hates to be big,
'T is he that inhabits the caves that you dig;
'T is he when you play with your soldiers of tin
That sides with the Frenchmen and never can win.

'T is he, when at night you go off to your bed,
Bids you go to your sleep and not trouble your head;
For wherever they're lying, in cupboard or shelf,
'T is he will take care of your playthings himself!

ROBERT LOUIS STEVENSON

COME AND PLAY
IN THE GARDEN

Little sister, come away,
And let us in the garden play,
For it is a pleasant day.
On the grass-plat let us sit,
Or, if you please, we'll play a bit,
And run about all over it.
But the fruit we will not pick,
For that would be a naughty trick,
And very likely make us sick.
Nor will we pluck the pretty flowers
That grow about the beds and bowers,
Because you know they are not ours.
We'll take the daisies, white and red,
Because mamma has often said
That we may gather them instead.
And much I hope we always may
Our very dear mamma obey,
And mind whatever she may say.

JANE TAYLOR

God writes the gospel not in the Bible alone,
but on trees, and flowers, and clouds, and stars.

MARTIN LUTHER

THE CUPBOARD

I know a little cupboard,
With a teeny tiny key,
And there's a jar of Lollipops
For me, me, me.

It has a little shelf, my dear,
As dark as dark can be,
And there's a dish of Banbury Cakes
For me, me, me.

I have a small fat grandmamma,
With a very slippery knee,
And she's Keeper of the Cupboard,
With the key, key, key.

And when I'm very good, my dear,
As good as good can be,
There's Banbury Cakes, and Lollipops
For me, me, me.

WALTER DE LA MARE

TO A BEE

Busy Bee, busy Bee, where are you going?
Down where the bluebells are budding and blowing,
There I shall find something hidden and sweet
That all little children are willing to eat!
Busy Bee, busy Bee, what will you do?
Put it into my pocket, and save it for you!

MAUDE KEARY

MY KINGDOM

Down by a shining water well
I found a very little dell,
　　No higher than my head.
The heather and the gorse about
In summer bloom were coming out,
　　Some yellow and some red.
I called the little pool a sea;
The little hills were big to me;
　　For I am very small.
I made a boat, I made a town,
I searched the caverns up and down,
　　And named them one and all.
And all about was mine, I said,
The little sparrows overhead,
　　The little minnows too.
This was the world and I was king;
For me the bees came by to sing,
　　For me the swallows flew.
I played, there were no deeper seas,
Nor any wider plains than these,
　　Nor other kings than me.

At last I heard my mother call
Out from the house at evenfall,
To call me home to tea.
And I must rise and leave my dell,
And leave my dimpled water well,
And leave my heather blooms.
Alas! and as my home I neared,
How very big my nurse appeared,
How great and cool the rooms!

ROBERT LOUIS STEVENSON

Every man's life is a fairy tale, written by God's fingers.

HANS CHRISTIAN ANDERSEN

I tell you the truth.
You must accept the kingdom of God
as a little child accepts things,
or you will never enter it.

MARK 10:15

CLOUDS

White sheep, white sheep
On a blue hill,
When the wind stops
You all stand still.
When the wind blows
You walk away slow.
White sheep, white sheep,
Where do you go?

CHRISTINA ROSSETTI

THE CLOUD

I bring fresh showers for the thirsting flowers,
From the seas and the streams;
I bear light shade for the leaves when laid
In their noonday dreams.
From my wings are shaken the dews that waken
The sweet buds every one,
When rocked to rest on their mother's breast,
As she dances about the sun.
I wield the flail of the lashing hail,
And whiten the green plains under,
And then again I dissolve it in rain,
And laugh as I pass in thunder.

PERCY BYSSHE SHELLEY

The heavens tell the glory of God.
And the skies announce what his hands have made.
Day after day they tell the story.
Night after night they tell it again.
They have no speech or words.
They don't make any sound to be heard.
But their message goes out through all the world.
It goes everywhere on earth.
PSALM 19:1–4

MY TREASURES

These nuts, that I keep in the back of the nest
Where all my lead soldiers are lying at rest,
Were gathered in autumn by nursie and me
In a wood with a well by the side of the sea.

This whistle was made (and how clearly it sounds!)
By the side of a field at the end of the grounds.
Of a branch of a plane, with a knife of my own—
It was nursie who made it, and nursie alone!

The stone, with the white and the yellow and gray,
We discovered I cannot tell *how* far away;
And I carried it back although weary and cold,
For though father denies it, I'm sure it is gold.

But of all of my treasures the last is the king,
For there's very few children possess such a thing;
And that is a chisel, both handle and blade,
Which a man who was really a carpenter made.

ROBERT LOUIS STEVENSON

46

LOOKING FORWARD

When I am grown to man's estate
I shall be very proud and great,
And tell the other girls and boys
Not to meddle with my toys.

ROBERT LOUIS STEVENSON

Praise God from whom all blessings flow!

BISHOP THOMAS KEN

BLOCK CITY

What are you able to build with your blocks?
Castles and palaces, temples and docks.
Rain may keep raining, and others go roam,
But I can be happy and building at home.
Let the sofa be mountains, the carpet be sea,
There I'll establish a city for me:
A kirk* and a mill and a palace beside,
And a harbor as well where my vessels may ride.

Great is the palace with pillar and wall,
A sort of a tower on the top of it all,
And steps coming down in an orderly way
To where my toy vessels lie safe in the bay.
This one is sailing and that one is moored:
Hark to the song of the sailors on board!
And see on the steps of my palace, the kings
Coming and going with presents and things!

Now I have done with it, down let it go!
All in a moment the town is laid low.
Block upon block lying scattered and free,
What is there left of my town by the sea?
Yet as I saw it, I see it again,
The kirk and the palace, the ships and the men,
And as long as I live and where'er I may be,
I'll always remember my town by the sea.

ROBERT LOUIS STEVENSON

* church

You made my whole being.
You formed me in my mother's body.
I praise you because you made me in an amazing
and wonderful way.
What you have done is wonderful.
I know this very well.

PSALM 139:13–14

THE WIND

I saw you toss the kites on high
And blow the birds about the sky;
And all around I heard you pass,
Like ladies' skirts across the grass—
    O wind, a-blowing all day long,
    O wind, that sings so loud a song!

I saw the different things you did,
But always you yourself you hid.
I felt you push, I heard you call,
I could not see yourself at all—
    O wind, a-blowing all day long,
    O wind, that sings so loud a song!

O you that are so strong and cold,
O blower, are you young or old?
Are you a beast of field and tree,
Or just a stronger child than me?
    O wind, a-blowing all day long,
    O wind, that sings so loud a song!

ROBERT LOUIS STEVENSON

WHO HAS SEEN THE WIND?

Who has seen the wind?
　　Neither I nor you:
But when the leaves hang trembling
　　The wind is passing thro'.

Who has seen the wind?
　　Neither you nor I:
But when the trees bow down their heads
　　The wind is passing by.

CHRISTINA ROSSETTI

LITTLE WIND

Little wind, blow on the hilltop;
Little wind, blow down the plain;
Little wind, blow up the sunshine;
Little wind, blow off the rain.

KATE GREENAWAY

*The wind blows where it wants to go.
You hear the wind blow. But you don't know where
the wind comes from or where it is going. It is the same
with every person who is born from the Spirit.*

JOHN 3:8

CHILD'S SONG

I have a garden of my own,
> Shining with flow'rs of ev'ry hue;
I loved it dearly while alone,
> But I shall love it more with you:
And there the golden bees shall come,
> In summertime at break of morn,
And wake us with their busy hum
> Around the Siha's fragrant thorn.

I have a fawn from Aden's land,
> On leafy buds and berries nurst,
And you shall feed him from your hand,
> Though he may start with fear at first.
And I will lead you where he lies
> For shelter in the noontide heat;
And you may touch his sleeping eyes,
> And feel his little silv'ry feet.

THOMAS MOORE

Come, my dear children,
Up is the sun,
Birds are all singing,
And morn has begun.

Up from the bed, Miss,
Out on the lea;
The horses are waiting
For you and for me!

MOTHER GOOSE

GOOD AND BAD CHILDREN

Children, you are very little,
And your bones are very brittle;
If you would grow great and stately,
You must try to walk sedately.

You must still be bright and quiet,
And content with simple diet;
And remain, through all bewild'ring,
Innocent and honest children.

Happy hearts and happy faces,
Happy play in grassy places—
That was how, in ancient ages,
Children grew to kings and sages.

But the unkind and the unruly,
And the sort who eat unduly,
They must never hope for glory—
Theirs is quite a different story!

Cruel children, crying babies,
All grow up as geese and gabies,
Hated, as their age increases,
By their nephews and their nieces.

ROBERT LOUIS STEVENSON

WHOLE DUTY OF CHILDREN

A child should always say what's true
And speak when he is spoken to,
And behave mannerly at table:
At least as far as he is able.

ROBERT LOUIS STEVENSON

Whatever work you do,

do your best.

ECCLESIASTES 9:10

THE SWING

How do you like to go up in a swing,
    Up in the air so blue?
Oh, I do think it the pleasantest thing
    Ever a child can do!

Up in the air and over the wall,
    Till I can see so wide,
Rivers and trees and cattle and all
    Over the countryside—

Till I look down on the garden green,
    Down on the roof so brown—
Up in the air I go flying again,
    Up in the air and down!

ROBERT LOUIS STEVENSON

Be full of joy in the Lord always.
I will say again, be full of joy.
PHILIPPIANS 4:4

LAUGHING SONG

When the green woods laugh with the voice of joy,
And the dimpling stream runs laughing by;
When the air does laugh with our merry wit,
And the green hill laughs with the noise of it;

When the meadows laugh with lively green,
And the grasshopper laughs in the merry scene,
When Mary and Susan and Emily
With their sweet round mouths sing "Ha, Ha, He!"

When the painted birds laugh in the shade,
Where our table with cherries and nuts is spread,
Come live and be merry, and join with me,
To sing the sweet chorus of "Ha, Ha, He!"

WILLIAM BLAKE

TIME TO RISE

A birdie with a yellow bill
Hopped upon the window sill,
Cocked his shining eye and said:
"Ain't you 'shamed, you sleepyhead?"

ROBERT LOUIS STEVENSON

HURT NO LIVING THING

Hurt no living thing:
Ladybird, nor butterfly,
Nor moth with dusty wing,
Nor cricket chirping cheerily,
Nor grasshopper so light of leap,
Nor dancing gnat, nor beetle fat,
Nor harmless worms that creep.

CHRISTINA ROSSETTI

THE LITTLE BIRD

Once I saw a little bird
Come hop, hop, hop,
And I cried, "Little bird,
Will you stop, stop, stop?"

I was going to the window
To say, "How do you do?"
But he shook his little tail
And away he flew.

MOTHER GOOSE

THE SWALLOW

Fly away, fly away over the sea,
Sun-loving swallow, for summer is done;
Come again, come again, come back to me,
Bringing the summer and bringing the sun.

CHRISTINA ROSSETTI

My heart is like a singing bird.

CHRISTINA ROSSETTI

WHEN YOU AND I GROW UP

When you and I
Grow up—Polly—
    I mean that you and me,
Shall go sailing in a big ship
    Right over all the sea.
We'll wait till we are older,
    For if we went today,
You know that we might lose ourselves,
    And never find the way.

KATE GREENAWAY

ON THE BRIDGE

If I could see a little fish—
That is what I just now wish!
I want to see his great round eyes
Always open in surprise.

I wish a water rat would glide
Slowly to the other side;
Or a dancing spider sit
On the yellow flags a bit.

I think I'll get some stones to throw
And watch the pretty circles show.
Or shall we sail a flower boat,
And watch it slowly—slowly float?

That's nice—because you never know
How far away it means to go;
And when tomorrow comes, you see,
It may be in the great wide sea.

KATE GREENAWAY

NEST EGGS

Birds all the sunny day
    Flutter and quarrel
Here in the arbor-like
    Tent of the laurel.

Here in the fork
    The brown nest is seated;
Four little blue eggs
    The mother keeps heated.

While we stand watching her,
    Staring like gabies,
Safe in each egg are the
    Bird's little babies.

Soon the frail eggs they shall
    Chip, and upspringing
Make all the April woods
    Merry with singing.

Younger than we are,
    O children, and frailer,
Soon in blue air they'll be,
    Singer and sailor.

We, so much older,
    Taller and stronger,
We shall look down on the
    Birdies no longer.

They shall go flying
    With musical speeches
High overhead in the
    Tops of the beeches.

In spite of our wisdom
    And sensible talking,
We on our feet must go
    Plodding and walking.

ROBERT LOUIS STEVENSON

Look at the birds.

They don't plant or harvest.

They don't save food in houses or barns.

But God takes care of them.

And you are worth much more than birds.

LUKE 12:24

THE SUMMER SUN SHONE ROUND ME

The summer sun shone round me,
The folded valley lay
In a stream of sun and odor,
That sultry summer day.

The tall trees stood in the sunlight
As still as still could be,
But the deep grass sighed and rustled
And bowed and beckoned me.

The deep grass moved and whispered
And bowed and brushed my face.
It whispered in the sunshine:
"The winter comes apace."

ROBERT LOUIS STEVENSON

64

FROM
HYMNS IN PROSE FOR CHILDREN

There is little need that I should tell you of God,

for every thing speaks of him.

Every field is like an open book;

every painted flower hath a lesson

written on its leaves.

Every murmuring brook hath a tongue;

a voice is in every whispering wind.

They all speak of him who made them;

they all tell us, he is very good.

We cannot see God, for he is invisible;

but we can see his works,

and worship his footsteps in the green sod.

ANNA LÆTITIA BARBAULD

Lord, your love reaches to the heavens.
Your loyalty goes to the skies.
PSALM 36:5

RAIN

The rain is raining all around,
It falls on field and tree,
It rains on the umbrellas here,
And on the ships at sea.

ROBERT LOUIS STEVENSON

Rain on the green grass,
And rain on the tree;
Rain on the housetop,
But not on me.

MOTHER GOOSE

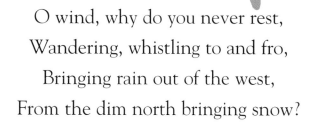

O wind, why do you never rest,
Wandering, whistling to and fro,
Bringing rain out of the west,
From the dim north bringing snow?

CHRISTINA ROSSETTI

Rain, Rain, go away;
Come again another day;
Little Johnny wants to play.

MOTHER GOOSE

I am putting my rainbow in the clouds.
It is the sign of the agreement
between me and the earth.

GENESIS 9:13

THE COCK CROWS IN THE MORN

The cock crows in the morn
To tell us to rise,
And he that lies late
Will never be wise:
For early to bed
And early to rise
Is the way to be healthy
And wealthy and wise.

MOTHER GOOSE

The Lord's love never ends.
His mercies never stop.
They are new every morning.
Lord, your loyalty is great.

LAMENTATIONS 3:22–23

THE COCK'S CLEAR VOICE INTO THE CLEARER AIR

The cock's clear voice into the clearer air
Where westward far I roam,
Mounts with a thrill of hope,
Falls with a sigh of home.

A rural sentry, he from farm and field
The coming morn descries,
And, mankind's bugler, wakes
The camp of enterprise.

He sings the morn upon the westward hills
Strange and remote and wild;
He sings it in the land
Where once I was a child.

He brings to me dear voices of the past
The old land and the years:
My father calls for me,
My weeping spirit hears.

Fife, fife, into the golden air, O bird,
And sing the morning in;
For the old days are past
And new days begin.

ROBERT LOUIS STEVENSON

COME,
MY LITTLE CHILDREN

Come, my little children, here are songs for you;
Some are short and some are long and all, all are new.
You must learn to sing them very small and clear,
Very true to time and tune and pleasing to the ear.

Mark the note that rises, mark the notes that fall.
Mark the time when broken, and the swing of it all.
So when night is come and you have gone to bed,
All the songs you love to sing shall echo in your head.

ROBERT LOUIS STEVENSON

I will make you brooches and toys for your delight
Of birdsong at morning and star shine at night.
I will make a palace fit for you and me,
Of green days in forests and blue days at sea.

ROBERT LOUIS STEVENSON

I will sing to the Lord all my life.
I will sing praises to my God as long as I live.
May my thoughts please him.
I am happy in the Lord.

PSALM 104:33–34

THE DUMB SOLDIER

When the grass was closely mown,
Walking on the lawn alone,
In the turf a hole I found
And hid a soldier underground.

Spring and daisies came apace;
Grasses hide my hiding place;
Grasses run like a green sea
O'er the lawn up to my knee.

Under grass alone he lies,
Looking up with leaden eyes,
Scarlet coat and pointed gun,
To the stars and to the sun.

When the grass is ripe like grain,
When the scythe is stoned again,
When the lawn is shaven clear,
Then my hole shall reappear.

I shall find him, never fear,
I shall find my grenadier;
But for all that's gone and come,
I shall find my soldier dumb.

He has lived, a little thing,
In the grassy woods of spring;
Done, if he could tell me true,
Just as I should like to do.

In the silence he has heard
Talking bee and ladybird,
And the butterfly has flown
O'er him as he lay alone.

Not a word will he disclose,
Not a word of all he knows.
I must lay him on the shelf,
And make up the tale myself.

ROBERT LOUIS STEVENSON

TO WILLIE AND HENRIETTA

If two may read aright
These rhymes of old delight
And house and garden play,
You two, my cousins, and you only, may.

You in a garden green
With me were king and queen,
Were hunter, soldier, tar,
And all the thousand things that children are.

Now in the elders' seat
We rest with quiet feet,
And from the window-bay
We watch the children, our successors, play.

"Time was," the golden head
Irrevocably said;
But time which none can bind,
While flowing fast away, leaves love behind.

ROBERT LOUIS STEVENSON

AUNTIE'S SKIRTS

Whenever Auntie moves around,
Her dresses make a curious sound;
They trail behind her up the floor,
And trundle after through the door.

ROBERT LOUIS STEVENSON

My true brothers and sisters and mother are those
who do the things that my Father in heaven wants.
MATTHEW 12:50

THE GARDENER

The gardener does not love to talk,
He makes me keep the gravel walk;
And when he puts his tools away,
He locks the door and takes the key.

Away behind the currant row
Where no one else but cook may go,
Far in the plots, I see him dig,
Old and serious, brown and big.

He digs the flowers, green, red and blue,
Nor wishes to be spoken to.
He digs the flowers and cuts the hay,
And never seems to want to play.

Silly gardener! summer goes,
And winter comes with pinching toes,
When in the garden bare and brown
You must lay your barrow down.

Well now, and while the summer stays,
To profit by these garden days,
O how much wiser you would be
To play at Indian wars with me!

ROBERT LOUIS STEVENSON

AUTUMN FIRES

In the other gardens
     And all up the vale,
From the autumn bonfires
     See the smoke trail!

Pleasant summer over
     And all the summer flowers,
The red fire blazes,
     The gray smoke towers.

Sing a song of seasons!
     Something bright in all!
Flowers in the summer,
     Fires in the fall!

ROBERT LOUIS STEVENSON

Then the Lord God planted a garden in the East,
in a place called Eden.
GENESIS 2:8

I praise the Lord because he guides me.
Even at night, I feel his leading.
PSALM 16:7

Day's
End

THE CHILDREN'S HOUR

Between the dark and the daylight,
    When the light is beginning to lower,
Comes a pause in the day's occupations
    That is known as the Children's Hour.

I hear in the chamber above me
    The patter of little feet,
The sound of a door that is opened,
    And voices soft and sweet.

From my study I see in the lamplight,
    Descending the broad hall stair,
Grave Alice and laughing Allegra,
    And Edith with golden hair.

A whisper, and then a silence;
    Yet I know by their merry eyes,
They are plotting and planning together
    To take me by surprise.

A sudden rush from the stairway,
    A sudden raid from the hall!
By three doors left unguarded
    They enter my castle wall!

They climb up into my turret,
    O'er the arms and back of my chair;
If I try to escape, they surround me;
    They seem to be everywhere.

They almost devour me with kisses,
    Their arms about me entwine,
Till I think of the Bishop of Bingen
    In his Mouse-Tower on the Rhine.

Do you think, O blue-eyed banditti,
    Because you have scaled the wall,
Such an old mustache as I am
    Is not a match for you all?

I have you fast in my fortress,
    And will not let you depart,
But put you down into the dungeon
    In the round-tower of my heart.

And there will I keep you forever,
    Yes, forever and a day,
Till the wall shall crumble to ruin,
    And moulder in dust away.

HENRY WADSWORTH LONGFELLOW

Everything on earth, shout with joy to God!

PSALM 66:1

BED IN SUMMER

In winter I get up at night
And dress by yellow candlelight.
In summer, quite the other way,
I have to go to bed by day.

I have to go to bed and see
The birds still hopping on the tree,
Or hear the grown-up people's feet
Still going past me in the street.

And does it not seem hard to you,
When all the sky is clear and blue,
And I should like so much to play,
To have to go to bed by day?

ROBERT LOUIS STEVENSON

NURSE'S SONG

When the voices of children are heard on the green,
And laughing is heard on the hill,
My heart is at rest within my breast,
And everything else is still.

"Then come home, my children, the sun is gone down,
And the dews of night arise;
Come, come, leave off play, and let us away
Till the morning appears in the skies."

"No, no, let us play, for it is yet day,
And we cannot go to sleep;
Besides, in the sky the little birds fly,
And the hills are all covered with sheep."

"Well, well, go and play till the light fades away,
And then go home to bed."
The little ones leaped and shouted and laughed
And all the hills echoèd.

WILLIAM BLAKE

YOUNG NIGHT THOUGHT

All night long and every night,
When my mamma puts out the light,
I see the people marching by,
As plain as day, before my eye.

Armies and emperors and kings,
All carrying different kinds of things,
And marching in so grand a way,
You never saw the like by day.

So fine a show was never seen,
At the great circus on the green;
For every kind of beast and man
Is marching in that caravan.

At first they move a little slow,
But still the faster on they go,
And still beside them close I keep
Until we reach the town of Sleep.

ROBERT LOUIS STEVENSON

SHADOW MARCH

All round the house is the jet-black night:
It stares through the windowpane;
It crawls in the corners, hiding from the light,
And it moves with the moving flame.

Now my little heart goes a-beating like a drum,
With the breath of the Bogie in my hair;
And all round the candle the crooked shadows come
And go marching along up the stair.

The shadow of the balusters, the shadow of the lamp,
The shadow of the child that goes to bed—
All the wicked shadows coming, tramp, tramp, tramp,
With the black night overhead.

ROBERT LOUIS STEVENSON

Lord, you give light to my lamp.
The Lord brightens the darkness around me.
2 SAMUEL 22:29

THE LAND OF NOD

From breakfast on through all the day
At home among my friends I stay;
But every night I go abroad
Afar into the Land of Nod.

All by myself I have to go,
With none to tell me what to do—
All alone beside the streams
And up the mountainsides of dreams.

The strangest things are there for me,
Both things to eat and things to see,
And many frightening sights abroad
Till morning in the Land of Nod.

Try as I like to find the way,
I never can get back by day,
Nor can remember plain and clear
The curious music that I hear.

ROBERT LOUIS STEVENSON

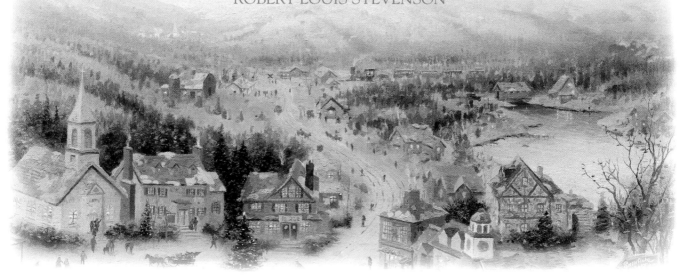

A DREAM

Last night when I was fast asleep,
Who do you think ran after me?
But A, B, C, each holding hands—
It was the strangest sight to see!

A danced a jig on nimble feet,
Fat B sat down upon the bed,
And C, to show what he could do,
Turned round and stood upon his head!

In blank surprise I stared at them—
How odd the dancing letters seemed!
And then I rubbed my eyes and woke,
And knew that I had only dreamed!

MAUDE KEARY

MY BED IS A BOAT

My bed is like a little boat;
Nurse helps me in when I embark;
She girds me in my sailor's coat
And starts me in the dark.

At night, I go on board and say
Good night to all my friends on shore;
I shut my eyes and sail away
And see and hear no more.

And sometimes things to bed I take,
As prudent sailors have to do:
Perhaps a slice of wedding cake,
Perhaps a toy or two.

All night across the dark we steer:
But when the day returns at last,
Safe in my room, beside the pier,
I find my vessel fast.

ROBERT LOUIS STEVENSON

SWEET AND LOW

Sweet and low, sweet and low,
Wind of the western sea,
Low, low, breathe and blow,
Wind of the western sea!
Over the rolling waters go,
Come from the dying moon, and blow,
Blow him again to me;
While my little one, while my pretty one, sleeps.

Sleep and rest, sleep and rest,
Father will come to thee soon;
Rest, rest, on mother's breast,
Father will come to thee soon;
Father will come to his babe in the nest,
Silver sails all out of the west
Under the silver moon;
Sleep, my little one, sleep, my pretty one, sleep.

ALFRED, LORD TENNYSON

Protect me, O Lord;
My boat is so small,
And your sea is so big.

TRADITIONAL BRETON PRAYER

WYNKEN, BLYNKEN, AND NOD

Wynken, Blynken, and Nod one night
      Sailed off in a wooden shoe—
Sailed on a river of crystal light,
      Into a sea of dew.
"Where are you going, and what do you wish?"
      The old moon asked the three.
"We have come to fish for the herring fish
      That live in this beautiful sea;
      Nets of silver and gold have we!"
          Said Wynken,
          Blynken,
          And Nod.

The old moon laughed and sang a song,
      As they rocked in the wooden shoe,
And the wind that sped them all night long
      Ruffled the waves of dew.
The little stars were the herring fish
      That lived in that beautiful sea—
"Now cast your nets wherever you wish—
      Never afeard are we";
      So cried the stars to the fishermen three:
          Wynken,
          Blynken,
          And Nod.

All night long their nets they threw
        To the stars in the twinkling foam—
Then down from the skies came the wooden shoe,
        Bringing the fishermen home;
'T was all so pretty a sail it seemed
        As if it could not be,
And some folks thought 't was a dream they'd dreamed
        Of sailing that beautiful sea—
        But I shall name you the fishermen three:
                Wynken,
                Blynken,
                And Nod.

Wynken and Blynken are two little eyes,
        And Nod is a little head,
And the wooden shoe that sailed the skies
        Is a wee one's trundle bed.
So shut your eyes while mother sings
        Of wonderful sights that be,
And you shall see the beautiful things
        As you rock in the misty sea,
        Where the old shoe rocked the fishermen three:
                Wynken,
                Blynken,
                And Nod.

EUGENE FIELD

I *love* to be warm by the red fireside,
I love to be wet with rain;
I love to be welcome at lamplit doors,
And leave the doors again.

ROBERT LOUIS STEVENSON

IN PORT

Last, to the chamber where I lie
My fearful footsteps patter nigh,
And come from out the cold and gloom
Into my warm and cheerful room.

There, safe arrived, we turn about
To keep the coming shadows out,
And close the happy door at last
On all the perils that we past.

Then, when mamma goes by to bed,
She shall come in with tiptoe tread,
And see me lying warm and fast
And in the Land of Nod at last.

ROBERT LOUIS STEVENSON

WINTER

Bread and milk for breakfast,
And woolen frocks to wear,
And a crumb for robin redbreast
On the cold days of the year.

CHRISTINA ROSSETTI

A CRADLE SONG

Golden slumbers kiss your eyes,
Smiles awake you when you rise.
Sleep, pretty wantons, do not cry,
And I will sing a lullaby:
Rock them, rock them, lullaby.

Care is heavy, therefore, sleep you;
You are care, and care must keep you.
Sleep, pretty wantons, do not cry,
And I will sing a lullaby:
Rock them, rock them, lullaby.

THOMAS DEKKER

GOOD NIGHT

Little baby, lay your head
On your pretty cradle bed;
Shut your eye-peeps, now the day
And the light are gone away;
All the clothes are tucked in tight;
Little baby dear, good night.

Yes, my darling, well I know
How the bitter wind doth blow;
And the winter's snow and rain
Patter on the windowpane;
But they cannot come in here,
To my little baby dear;

For the window shutteth fast,
Till the stormy night is past;
And the curtains warm are spread
Round about her cradle bed.
So till morning shineth bright,
Little baby dear, good night.

JANE TAYLOR

Those who are pure in their thinking are happy.
They will be with God.
MATTHEW 5:8

ESCAPE AT BEDTIME

The lights from the parlor and kitchen shone out
    Through the blinds and the windows and bars;
And high overhead and all moving about,
    There were thousands of millions of stars.
There ne'er were such thousands of leaves on a tree,
    Nor of people in church or the Park,
As the crowds of the stars that looked down upon me,
    And that glittered and winked in the dark.
The Dog, and the Plough, and the Hunter, and all,
    And the star of the sailor, and Mars,
These shone in the sky, and the pail by the wall,
    Would be half full of water and stars.
They saw me at last, and they chased me with cries,
    And they soon had me packed into bed;
But the glory kept shining and bright in my eyes,
    And the stars going round in my head.

ROBERT LOUIS STEVENSON

96

Star light, star bright,
First star I see tonight,
I wish I may, I wish I might,
Have the wish I wish tonight.

MOTHER GOOSE

After the sun is down, and the west faded,
the heavens begin to fill with stars.

ROBERT LOUIS STEVENSON

He counts the stars and names each one.
PSALM 147:4

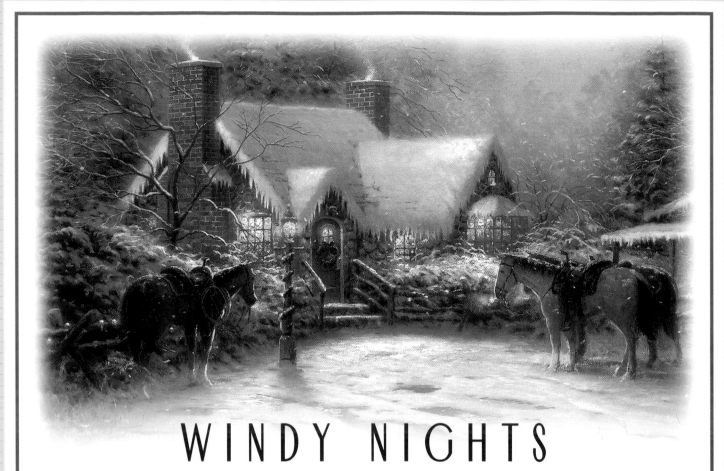

WINDY NIGHTS

Whenever the moon and stars are set,
Whenever the wind is high,
All night long in the dark and wet,
A man goes riding by.
Late in the night when the fires are out,
Why does he gallop and gallop about?

Whenever the trees are crying aloud,
And ships are tossed at sea,
By, on the highway, low and loud,
By at the gallop goes he;
By at the gallop he goes, and then
By he comes back at the gallop again.

ROBERT LOUIS STEVENSON

THE SUN'S TRAVELS

The sun is not a-bed, when I
At night upon my pillow lie;
Still round the earth his way he takes,
And morning after morning makes.

While here at home, in shining day,
We round the sunny garden play,
Each little Indian sleepyhead
Is being kissed and put to bed.

And when at eve I rise from tea,
Day dawns beyond the Atlantic Sea,
And all the children in the West
Are getting up and being dressed.

ROBERT LOUIS STEVENSON

He made the moon and stars to rule the night.
His love continues forever.
PSALM 136:9

THE LAMPLIGHTER

My tea is nearly ready and the sun has left the sky;
It's time to take the window to see Leerie going by;
For every night at teatime and before you take your seat,
With lantern and with ladder he comes posting up the street.

Now Tom would be a driver and Maria go to sea,
And my papa's a banker and as rich as he can be;
But I, when I am stronger and can choose what I'm to do,
O Leerie, I'll go round at night and light the lamps with you!

For we are very lucky, with a lamp before the door,
And Leerie stops to light it as he lights so many more;
And O! before you hurry by with ladder and with light,
O Leerie, see a little child and nod to him tonight!

ROBERT LOUIS STEVENSON

Lord, keep us safe this night,
Secure from all our fears;
May angels guard us while we sleep,
Till morning light appears.

JOHN LELAND

This little light of mine,
I'm gonna let it shine.
This little light of mine,
I'm gonna let it shine.
This little light of mine,
I'm gonna let it shine.
Let it shine,
Let it shine,
Let it shine.

UNKNOWN

THE MOON

The moon has a face like the clock in the hall;
She shines on thieves on the garden wall,
On streets and fields and harbor quays,
And birdies asleep in the forks of the trees.

The squalling cat and the squeaking mouse,
The howling dog by the door of the house,
The bat that lies in bed at noon,
All love to be out by the light of the moon.

But all of the things that belong to the day
Cuddle to sleep to be out of her way;
And flowers and children close their eyes
Till up in the morning the sun shall arise.

ROBERT LOUIS STEVENSON

I SEE THE MOON

I see the moon,
And the moon sees me;
God bless the moon,
And God bless me.

OLD NURSERY RHYME

WHO BLOWS YOU OUT?

O little round and yellow moon,
Why have you lit yourself so soon?
Jane won't bring in the lamp for me,
She says it's light enough to see!

Perhaps you did not know the time,
But don't you hear the church clocks chime?
Who blows you out, I wonder, when
The shining day comes back again?

MAUDE KEARY

I look at the heavens, which you made with your hands.
I see the moon and stars, which you created.
PSALM 8:3

AWAY IN A MANGER

Away in a manger,
No crib for a bed,
The little Lord Jesus
Lay down his sweet head;
The stars in the heavens
Looked down where he lay,
The little Lord Jesus
Asleep in the hay.

The cattle are lowing,
The poor baby wakes,
But little Lord Jesus
No crying he makes.
I love thee, Lord Jesus,
Look down from the sky,
And stay by my cradle
Till morning is nigh.

MARTIN LUTHER

Angels at the foot,
And Angels at the head,
And like a curly little lamb
My pretty babe in bed.

CHRISTINA ROSSETTI

ANGELS WATCHING OVER ME

All night, all day,
Angels watching over me, my Lord.
All night, all day,
Angels watching over me.

Sun is a-setting in the West;
Angels watching over me, my Lord.
Sleep my child, take your rest;
Angels watching over me.

All night, all day,
Angels watching over me, my Lord.
All night, all day,
Angels watching over me.

UNKNOWN

GOOD NIGHT

When the bright lamp is carried in,
The sunless hours again begin;
O'er all without, in field and lane,
The haunted night returns again.

Now we behold the embers flee
About the firelit hearth; and see
Our faces painted as we pass,
Like pictures, on the window glass.

Must we to bed, indeed? Well then,
Let us arise and go like men,
And face with an undaunted tread
The long, black passage up to bed.

Farewell, O brother, sister, sire!
O pleasant party round the fire!
The songs you sing, the tales you tell,
Till far tomorrow, fare ye well!

ROBERT LOUIS STEVENSON

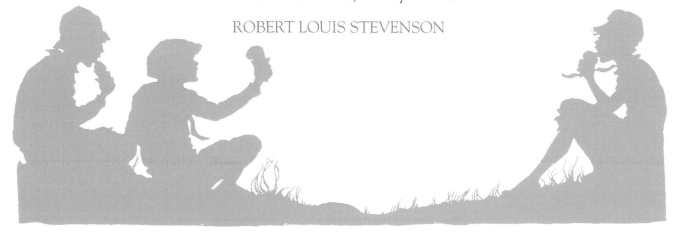

LITTLE FOLK

Little folks, little folks,
    Now then for bed!
A pillow is waiting,
    For each little head.

Sleep all the night,
    And wake in the morn;
Robert shall sound
    The call on his horn.

MOTHER GOOSE

TWILIGHT

The shadows deepen so you cannot see
Within the corners of the nursery;
Across the ceiling dim they dance and leap,
And stealthily along the floor they creep,
Only the teacups standing on the table
Bear each a shining fleck, a red fire label.

MAUDE KEARY

NIGHT AND DAY

When the golden day is done,
    Through the closing portal,
Child and garden, flower and sun,
    Vanish all things mortal.

As the blinding shadows fall,
    As the rays diminish,
Under the evening's cloak, they all
    Roll away and vanish.

Garden darkened, daisy shut,
    Child in bed, they slumber—
Glowworm in the highway rut,
    Mice among the lumber.

In the darkness houses shine,
    Parents move with candles;
Till on all, the night divine
    Turns the bedroom handles.

Till at last the day begins
    In the east a-breaking,
In the hedges and the whins
    Sleeping birds a-waking.

In the darkness shapes of things,
    Houses, trees, and hedges
Clearer grow; and sparrow's wings
    Beat on window ledges.

These shall wake the yawning maid;
    She the door shall open—
Finding dew on garden glade
    And the morning broken.

> *Our Lord has written the promise*
> *of the resurrection not in books alone,*
> *but in every leaf in springtime.*
> MARTIN LUTHER

There my garden grows again
    Green and rosy painted,
As at eve behind the pane
    From my eyes it fainted.

Just as it was shut away,
    Toy-like, in the even,
Here I see it glow with day
    Under glowing heaven.

Every path and every plot,
    Every bush of roses,
Every blue forget-me-not
    Where the dew reposes,

"Up!" they cry, "the day is come
    On the smiling valleys:
We have beat the morning drum;
    Playmate, join your allies!"

ROBERT LOUIS STEVENSON

109

THE STAR

Twinkle, twinkle, little star,
How I wonder what you are!
Up above the world so high,
Like a diamond in the sky.

When the blazing sun is gone,
When he nothing shines upon,
Then you show your little light,
Twinkle, twinkle, all the night.

Then the traveler in the dark
Thanks you for your tiny spark;
He could not see which way to go,
If you did not twinkle so.

In the dark blue sky you keep,
And often through my curtains peep,
For you never shut your eye
Till the sun is in the sky.

As your bright and tiny spark
Lights the traveler in the dark,
Though I know not what you are,
Twinkle, twinkle, little star.

JANE TAYLOR

What do the stars do
Up in the sky,
Higher than the wind can blow
Or the clouds can fly?

Each star in its own glory
Circles, circles still;
As it was lit to shine and set,
And do its Maker's will.

CHRISTINA ROSSETTI

COME TO THE WINDOW

Come to the window,

My baby, with me,

And look at the stars

That shine on the sea!

There are two little stars

That play at bo-peep

With two little fish

Far down in the deep;

And two little frogs

Cry neap, neap, neap;

I see a dear baby

That should be asleep.

MOTHER GOOSE

LULLABY

Lullaby, oh lullaby!
Flowers are closed and lambs are sleeping;
Lullaby, oh lullaby!
Stars are up, the moon is peeping;
Lullaby, oh lullaby!
While the birds are silence keeping,
Lullaby, oh lullaby!
Sleep, my baby, fall a-sleeping,
Lullaby, oh lullaby!

CHRISTINA ROSSETTI

GOOD NIGHT

Good night! Good night!
Far flies the light;
But still God's love
Shall flame above,
Making all bright.
Good night! Good night!

VICTOR HUGO

Now I lay me down to sleep.
I pray Thee, Lord, my soul to keep.
Your love be with me through the night
And wake me with the morning light.

TRADITIONAL

Wonders of Childhood

The little child began to grow up. He became
stronger and wiser, and God's blessings were with him.

LUKE 2:40

THE LITTLE LAND

When at home alone I sit
And am very tired of it,
I have just to shut my eyes
To go sailing through the skies—
To go sailing far away
To the pleasant Land of Play;

Where the clover tops are trees,
And the rain pools are the seas,
And the leaves like little ships
Sail about on tiny trips;
And above the daisy tree
        Through the grasses,
High o'erhead the Bumble Bee
        Hums and passes.

In that forest to and fro
I can wander, I can go;
See the spider and the fly,
And the ants go marching by
Carrying parcels with their feet
Down the green and grassy street.
I can in the sorrel sit
Where the ladybird alit.
I can climb the jointed grass;
        And on high
See the greater swallows pass
        In the sky,
And the round sun rolling by
Heeding no such things as I.

Through that forest I can pass
Till, as in a looking glass,
Humming fly and daisy tree
And my tiny self I see,
Painted very clear and neat
On the rain pool at my feet.
Should a leaflet come to land
Drifting near to where I stand,
Straight I'll board that tiny boat
Round the rain-pool sea to float.

Little thoughtful creatures sit
On the grassy coasts of it;
Little things with lovely eyes
See me sailing with surprise.
Some are clad in armor green—
(These have sure to battle been!)—
Some are pied with ev'ry hue,
Black and crimson, gold and blue;
Some have wings and swift are gone;—
But they all look kindly on.

When my eyes I once again
Open, and see all things plain:
High bare walls, great bare floor;
Great big knobs on drawer and door;
Great big people perched on chairs,
Stitching tucks and mending tears,
Each a hill that I could climb,
And talking nonsense all the time—
        O dear me,
        That I could be
A sailor on the rain-pool sea,
A climber in the clover tree,
And just come back, a sleepyhead,
Late at night to go to bed.

ROBERT LOUIS STEVENSON

DUCK'S DITTY

All along the backwater,
Through the rushes tall,
Ducks are a-dabbling,
Up tails all!

Ducks' tails, drakes' tails,
Yellow feet a-quiver,
Yellow bills all out of sight
Busy in the river!

Slushy green undergrowth
Where the roach swim—
Here we keep our larder,
Cool and full and dim!

Every one for what he likes!
We like to be
Heads down, tails up,
Dabbling free!

High in the blue above
Swifts whirl and call—
We are down a-dabbling
Up tails all!

KENNETH GRAHAME

I saw a ship a-sailing,
A-sailing on the sea;
And, oh! it was all laden
With pretty things for thee!

There were comfits in the cabin,
And apples in the hold;
The sails were made of silk,
And the masts were made of gold.

The four-and-twenty sailors
That stood between the decks,
Were four-and-twenty white mice
With chains about their necks.

The captain was a duck,
With a packet on his back;
And when the ship began to move,
The captain said, "Quack! Quack!"

MOTHER GOOSE

FOREIGN LANDS

Up into the cherry tree
Who should climb but little me?
I held the trunk with both my hands
And looked abroad on foreign lands.

I saw the next-door garden lie,
Adorned with flowers before my eye,
And many pleasant places more
That I had never seen before.

I saw the dimpling river pass
And be the sky's blue looking glass;
The dusty roads go up and down
With people tramping in to town.

If I could find a higher tree
Farther and farther I should see,
To where the grown-up river slips
Into the sea among the ships,

To where the roads on either hand
Lead onward into fairy land,
Where all the children dine at five,
And all the playthings come alive.

ROBERT LOUIS STEVENSON

FROM
HYMNS IN PROSE FOR CHILDREN

Many kingdoms, and countries full of people, and islands, and large continents, and different climates, make up this whole world—God governeth it. The people swarm upon the face of it like ants upon a hillock: some are black with the hot sun; some cover themselves with furs against the sharp cold; some drink of the fruit of the vine; some the pleasant milk of the cocoa nut; and others quench their thirst with the running stream.

All are God's family; he knoweth every one of them, as a shepherd knoweth his flock: they pray to him in different languages, but he understandeth them all; he heareth them all; he taketh care of all; none are so great, that he cannot punish them; none are so mean, that he will not protect them.

ANNA LÆTITIA BARBAULD

*"I will give peace, real peace,
to those far and near. And I will
heal them," says the Lord.*
ISAIAH 57:19

THE DUEL

The gingham dog and the calico cat
Side by side on the table sat;
'T was half-past twelve, and (what do you think!)
Nor one nor t' other had slept a wink!
    The old Dutch clock and the Chinese plate
    Appeared to know as sure as fate
There was going to be a terrible spat.
    (I wasn't there; I simply state
    What was told to me by the Chinese plate!)

The gingham dog went "Bow-wow-wow!"
And the calico cat replied "Mee-ow!"
The air was littered, an hour or so,
With bits of gingham and calico,
    While the old Dutch clock in the chimney-place
    Up with its hands before its face,
For it always dreaded a family row!
    (Now mind: I'm only telling you
    What the old Dutch clock declares is true!)

The Chinese plate looked very blue,
And wailed, "Oh, dear! what shall we do!"
But the gingham dog and the calico cat
Wallowed this way and tumbled that,
    Employing every tooth and claw
    In the awfullest way you ever saw—
And, oh! how the gingham and calico flew!
    (Don't fancy I exaggerate—
    I got my news from the Chinese plate!)

Next morning, where the two had sat
They found no trace of dog or cat;
And some folks think unto this day
That burglars stole that pair away!
    But the truth about the cat and pup
    Is this: they ate each other up!
Now what do you really think of that!
    (The old Dutch clock it told me so,
    And that is how I came to know.)

EUGENE FIELD

AT THE SEASIDE

When I was down beside the sea
A wooden spade they gave to me
To dig the sandy shore.
My holes were empty like a cup,
In every hole the sea came up,
Till it could come no more.

ROBERT LOUIS STEVENSON

BENEATH THE SEA

Were I a fish beneath the sea,
Shell-paved and pearl-brocaded,
Would you come down and live with me,
In groves by coral shaded?

No washing would we have to do;
Our cushions should be sponges—
And many a great ship's envious crew
Should watch our merry plunges!

MAUDE KEARY

Let the skies rejoice and the earth be glad.
Let people everywhere say, "The Lord is king!"
Let the sea and everything in it shout.
Let the fields and everything in them show their joy.
1 CHRONICLES 16:31–32

MY SHIP AND I

O it's I that am the captain of a tidy little ship,
　　Of a ship that goes a-sailing on the pond;
And my ship it keeps a-turning all around and all about;
But when I'm a little older, I shall find the secret out
　　How to send my vessel sailing on beyond.

For I mean to grow as little as the dolly at the helm,
　　And the dolly I intend to come alive;
And with him beside to help me, it's a-sailing I shall go,
It's a-sailing on the water, when the jolly breezes blow,
　　And the vessel goes a divie-divie-dive.

O it's then you'll see me sailing through the rushes and the reeds,
　　And you'll hear the water singing at the prow;
For beside the dolly sailor, I'm to voyage and explore,
To land upon the island where no dolly was before,
　　And to fire the penny cannon in the bow.

ROBERT LOUIS STEVENSON

SINGING

Of speckled eggs the birdie sings
And nests among the trees;
The sailor sings of ropes and things
In ships upon the seas.

The children sing in far Japan,
The children sing in Spain;
The organ with the organ man
Is singing in the rain.

ROBERT LOUIS STEVENSON

MARY'S LAMB

Mary had a little lamb,
 Its fleece was white as snow,
And everywhere that Mary went
 The lamb was sure to go;

He followed her to school one day—
 That was against the rule,
It made the children laugh and play
 To see a lamb at school.

And so the teacher turned him out,
 But still he lingered near,
And waited patiently about,
 Till Mary did appear.

"What makes the lamb love Mary so?"
 The little children cry;
"Oh, Mary loves the lamb, you know,"
 The teacher did reply.

SARAH JOSEPHA HALE

THE SQUIRREL

Whisky, frisky,
Hippity hop.
Up he goes
To the treetop!

Whirly, twirly,
Round and round,
Down he scampers
To the ground.

Furly, curly,
What a tail!
Tall as a feather,
Broad as a sail!

Where's his supper?
In the shell,
Snappity, crackity,
Out it fell!

ANONYMOUS

The Lord takes care of his people like a shepherd.
He gathers the people like lambs in his arms.
ISAIAH 40:11

THE LAND OF STORYBOOKS

At evening, when the lamp is lit,
Around the fire my parents sit;
They sit at home and talk and sing,
And do not play at anything.

Now, with my little gun, I crawl
All in the dark along the wall,
And follow round the forest track
Away behind the sofa back.

There, in the night, where none can spy,
All in my hunter's camp I lie,
And play at books that I have read
Till it is time to go to bed.

These are the hills, these are the woods,
These are my starry solitudes;
And there the river by whose brink
The roaring lions come to drink.

I see the others far away
As if in firelit camp they lay,
And I, like to an Indian scout,
Around their party prowled about.

So, when my nurse comes in for me,
Home I return across the sea,
And go to bed with backward looks
At my dear land of Storybooks.

ROBERT LOUIS STEVENSON

THE SUGARPLUM TREE

Have you ever heard of the Sugarplum Tree?
'T is a marvel of great renown!
It blooms on the shore of the Lollipop Sea
In the garden of Shuteye Town;
The fruit that it bears is so wondrously sweet
(As those who have tasted it say)
That good little children have only to eat
Of that fruit to be happy next day.

When you've got to the tree, you would have a hard time
To capture the fruit which I sing;
The tree is so tall that no person could climb
To the boughs where the sugarplums swing!
But up in that tree sits a chocolate cat,
And a gingerbread dog prowls below—
And this is the way you contrive to get at
Those sugarplums tempting you so:

You say but the word to that gingerbread dog
And he barks with such terrible zest
That the chocolate cat is at once all agog,
As her swelling proportions attest.
And the chocolate cat goes cavorting around
From this leafy limb unto that,
And the sugarplums tumble, of course, to the ground—
Hurrah for that chocolate cat!

There are marshmallows, gumdrops, and peppermint canes
With stripings of scarlet or gold,
And you carry away of the treasure that rains
As much as your apron can hold!
So come, little child, cuddle closer to me
In your dainty white nightcap and gown,
And I'll rock you away to that Sugarplum Tree
In the garden of Shuteye Town.

EUGENE FIELD

WHEN I GROW UP

When I grow up I mean to go
Where all the biggest rivers flow,
And take a ship and sail around
The Seven Seas until I've found
Robinson Crusoe's famous isle,
And there I'll land and stay a while,
And see how it would feel to be
Lord on an island in the sea.

When I grow up I mean to rove
Through orange and palmetto grove,
To drive a sledge across the snow
Where great explorers go,
To hunt for treasures hid of old
By buccaneers and pirates bold,
And see if somewhere there may be
A mountain no one's climbed but me.

When I grow up I mean to do
The things I've always wanted to;
I don't see why grown people stay
At home when they could be away.

RUPERT SARGENT HOLLAND

PIRATE STORY

Three of us afloat in the meadow by the swing,
    Three of us aboard in the basket on the lea.
Winds are in the air, they are blowing in the spring,
    And waves are on the meadow like the waves
        there are at sea.

Where shall we adventure today that we're afloat,
    Wary of the weather and steering by a star?
Shall it be to Africa, a-steering of the boat,
    To Providence, or Babylon, or off to Malabar?

Hi! but here's a squadron a-rowing on the sea—
    Cattle on the meadow a-charging with a roar!
Quick, and we'll escape them, they're as mad as they can be,
    The wicket is the harbor and the garden is the shore.

ROBERT LOUIS STEVENSON

When Christ came into my life,
I came about like a well-handled ship.

ROBERT LOUIS STEVENSON

THE OWL AND THE PUSSYCAT

The Owl and the Pussycat went to sea
    In a beautiful pea-green boat:
They took some honey, and plenty of money
    Wrapped up in a five-pound note.
The Owl looked up to the stars above,
    And sang to a small guitar,
"O lovely Pussy, O Pussy, my love,
    What a beautiful Pussy you are,
        You are,
        You are!
What a beautiful Pussy you are!"

Pussy said to the Owl, "You elegant fowl,
    How charmingly sweet you sing!
Oh! let us be married; too long we have tarried:
    But what shall we do for a ring?"
They sailed away, for a year and a day,
    To the land where the bong-tree grows;
And there in a wood a Piggy-wig stood,
    With a ring at the end of his nose,
        His nose,
        His nose,
With a ring at the end of his nose.

"Dear Pig, are you willing to sell for one shilling
    Your ring?" Said the Piggy, "I will."
So they took it away, and were married next day
    By the Turkey who lives on the hill.
They dined on mince and slices of quince,
    Which they ate with a runcible spoon;
And hand in hand, on the edge of the sand
    They danced by the light of the moon,
        The moon,
        The moon,
They danced by the light of the moon.

EDWARD LEAR

THE CARELESS KITTENS

Three little kittens, they lost their mittens,
And they began to cry,
"Oh, Mother dear, we sadly fear
That we have lost our mittens."
"What! lost your mittens, you naughty kittens!
Then you shall have no pie."
Mee-ow, mee-ow, mee-ow.
"No, you shall have no pie."

The three little kittens, they found their mittens,
And they began to cry,
"Oh, Mother dear, see here, see here,
Our mittens we have found."
"Put on your mittens, you silly kittens,
And you shall have some pie."
Purr-r, purr-r, purr-r.
"Oh, let us have some pie."

NURSERY RHYME

A DOG AND A CAT
WENT OUT TOGETHER

A dog and a cat went out together,

To see some friends just out of town;

Said the cat to the dog,

"What d'ye think of the weather?"

"I think, ma'am, the rain will come down;

But don't be alarmed, for I've an umbrella

That will shelter us both," said this amiable fellow.

MOTHER GOOSE

A VISIT FROM THE SEA

Far from the loud sea beaches
    Where he goes fishing and crying,
Here in the inland garden
    Why is the seagull flying?

Here are no fish to dive for;
    Here is the corn and lea;
Here are the green trees rustling.
    Hie away home to sea!

Fresh is the river water
    And quiet among the rushes;
This is no home for the seagull
    But for the rooks and thrushes.

Pity the bird that has wandered!
    Pity the sailor ashore!
Hurry him home to the ocean,
    Let him come here no more!

High on the sea-cliff ledges
    The white gulls are trooping and crying,
Here among the rooks and roses,
    Why is the seagull flying?

ROBERT LOUIS STEVENSON

THE HORSES OF THE SEA

The horses of the sea
Rear a foaming crest,
But the horses of the land
Serve us the best.

The horses of the land
Munch corn and clover,
While the foaming sea horses
Toss and turn over.

CHRISTINA ROSSETTI

*Then God said, "Let the water be filled with living things.
And let birds fly in the air above the earth."*
GENESIS 1:20

WHERE GO THE BOATS?

Dark brown is the river,
    Golden is the sand.
It flows along for ever,
    With trees on either hand.

Green leaves a-floating,
    Castles of the foam,
Boats of mine a-boating—
    Where will all come home?

On goes the river
    And out past the mill,
Away down the valley,
    Away down the hill.

Away down the river,
    A hundred miles or more,
Other little children
    Shall bring my boats ashore.

ROBERT LOUIS STEVENSON

RIVER, RIVER

River, river, running through the land,
Are you a traveler over foreign sand?
Are you a carrier from town to town,
River, river, as you hurry down?

Yes, I'm a carrier from town to town:
Here are ships with white sails, there are boats with brown,
What shall they bring you, what will you send?
I'll be your carrier to the land's end.

MAUDE KEARY

SUMMER SUN

Great is the sun, and wide he goes
Through empty heaven without repose;
And in the blue and glowing days
More thick than rain he showers his rays.

Though closer still the blinds we pull
To keep the shady parlor cool,
Yet he will find a chink or two
To slip his golden fingers through.

The dusty attic spider-clad
He, through the keyhole, maketh glad;
And through the broken edge of tiles,
Into the laddered hayloft smiles.

Meantime his golden face around
He bares to all the garden ground,
And sheds a warm and glittering look
Among the ivy's inmost nook.

Above the hills, along the blue,
Round the bright air with footing true,
To please the child, to paint the rose,
The gardener of the World, he goes.

ROBERT LOUIS STEVENSON

THANKSGIVING DAY

Over the river and through the wood,
   To grandfather's house we go;
     The horse knows the way
     To carry the sleigh
   Through the white and
     drifted snow.

Over the river and through the wood,
   Oh, how the wind does blow!
     It stings the toes
     And bites the nose,
   As over the ground we go.

Over the river and through the wood,
   To have a first-rate play.
     Hear the bells ring,
     "Ting-a-ling-ding!"
   Hurrah for Thanksgiving Day!

Over the river and through the wood,
   Trot fast, my dapple-gray!
     Spring over the ground,
     Like a hunting hound!
   For this is Thanksgiving Day.

Over the river and through the wood,
   And straight through the
     barnyard gate.
     We seem to go
     Extremely slow,—
   It is so hard to wait!

Over the river and through the wood,
   Now grandmother's cap I spy!
     Hurrah for the fun!
     Is the pudding done?
   Hurrah for the pumpkin pie!

LYDIA MARIA CHILD

The city mouse lives in a house;—
The garden mouse lives in a bower,
He's friendly with the frogs and toads,
And sees the pretty plants in flower.

The city mouse eats bread and cheese;—
The garden mouse eats what he can;
We will not grudge him seeds and stalks,
Poor little timid furry man.

CHRISTINA ROSSETTI

TWINKLE, TWINKLE, LITTLE BAT!

Twinkle, twinkle, little bat!
How I wonder what you're at!
Up above the world you fly,
Like a tea tray in the sky.
Twinkle, twinkle—

LEWIS CARROLL

THE PURPLE COW

I never saw a Purple Cow,
I never hope to see one;
But I can tell you, anyhow,
I'd rather see one than be one.

GELETT BURGESS

THERE WAS AN OLD MAN

There was an Old Man who said, "How
Shall I flee from this horrible Cow?
I will sit on this stile, and continue to smile,
Which may soften the heart of that Cow."

EDWARD LEAR

A good laugh is sunshine in a house.

WILLIAM MAKEPEACE THACKERAY

TRAVELS

I should like to rise and go
Where the golden apples grow;—
Where below another sky
Parrot islands anchored lie,
And, watched by cockatoos and goats,
Lonely Crusoes building boats;—
Where in sunshine reaching out
Eastern cities, miles about,
Are with mosque and minaret
Among sandy gardens set,
And the rich goods from near and far
Hang for sale in the bazaar;—
Where the Great Wall round China goes,
And on one side the desert blows,
And with bell and voice and drum,
Cities on the other hum;—
Where are forests, hot as fire,
Wide as England, tall as a spire,
Full of apes and cocoa nuts
And the negro hunters' huts;—
Where the knotty crocodile
Lies and blinks in the Nile,
And the red flamingo flies

Hunting fish before his eyes;—
Where in jungles near and far,
Man-devouring tigers are,
Lying close and giving ear
Lest the hunt be drawing near,
Or a comer-by be seen
Swinging in a palanquin:—
Where among the desert sands
Some deserted city stands,
All its children, sweep and prince,
Grown to manhood ages since,
Not a foot in street or house,
Not a stir of child or mouse,
And when kindly falls the night,
In all the town no spark of light.
There I'll come when I'm a man
With a camel caravan;
Light a fire in the gloom
Of some dusty dining room;
See the pictures on the walls,
Heroes, fights and festivals;
And in a corner find the toys
Of the old Egyptian boys.

ROBERT LOUIS STEVENSON

Jesus said, "Come follow me.
I will make you fishermen for men."

MATTHEW 4:19

THE BUTTERFLY'S

Come take up your hats, and away let us haste,
To the Butterfly's Ball, and the Grasshopper's Feast.
The trumpeter Gadfly has summoned the crew,
And the revels are now only waiting for you.

On the smooth-shaven grass by the side of a wood,
Beneath a broad oak which for ages has stood,
See the children of earth and the tenants of air,
For an evening's amusement together repair.

And there came the Beetle, so blind and so black,
Who carried the Emmet, his friend, on his back.
And there came the Gnat, and the Dragonfly too,
And all their relations, green, orange, and blue.

And there came the Moth, with her plumage of down,
And the Hornet, with jacket of yellow and brown;
Who with him the Wasp, his companion, did bring,
But they promised that evening, to lay by their sting.

Then the sly little Dormouse crept out of his hole,
And led to the feast his blind cousin the Mole.
And the Snail, with his horns peeping out of his shell,
Came, fatigued with the distance, the length of an ell.

BALL

A mushroom their table, and on it was laid
A water-dock leaf, which a tablecloth made.
The viands were various, to each of their taste,
And the Bee brought the honey to sweeten the feast.

With steps most majestic the Snail did advance,
And he promised the gazers a minuet to dance;
But they all laughed so loud that he drew in his head,
And went in his own little chamber to bed.

Then, as evening gave way to the shadows of night,
Their watchman, the Glowworm, came out with his light.
So home let us hasten, while yet we can see;
For no watchman is waiting for you and for me.

WILLIAM ROSCOE

Dear Father,
Hear and bless
Thy beasts and singing birds.
And guard with tenderness
Small things that have no words.

UNKNOWN

LOOKING GLASS RIVER

Smooth it slides upon its travel,
  Here a wimple, there a gleam—
    O the clean gravel!
    O the smooth stream!

Sailing blossoms, silver fishes,
  Paven pools as clear as air—
    How a child wishes
    To live down there!

We can see our colored faces
  Floating on the shaken pool
    Down in cool places,
    Dim and very cool;

Till a wind or water wrinkle,
  Dipping marten, plumping trout,
    Spreads in a twinkle
    And blots all out.

See the rings pursue each other;
  All below grows black as night,
    Just as if mother
    Had blown out the light!

Patience, children, just a minute—
  See the spreading circles die;
    The stream and all in it
    Will clear by-and-by.

ROBERT LOUIS STEVENSON

THE CAREFUL ANGLER

CHOSE HIS NOOK

The careful angler chose his nook

At morning by the lilied brook,

And all the noon his rod he plied

By that romantic riverside.

Soon as the evening hours decline

Tranquilly he'll return to dine,

And, breathing forth a pious wish,

Will cram his belly full of fish.

ROBERT LOUIS STEVENSON

You made the moon to mark the seasons.

And the sun always knows when to set.

PSALM 104:19

As round as an apple, as deep as a cup,
And all the king's horses can't pull it up.

Higher than a house,
Higher than a tree,
Oh! whatever can it be?

Lives in winter,
Dies in summer,
And grows with its roots upward!

There was a little green house,
And in the little green house
There was a little brown house,
And in the little brown house
There was a little yellow house,
And in the little yellow house
There was a little white house,
And in the little white house
There was a little heart.

ANSWERS
a well, a star, an icicle, a walnut

A pin has a head, but has no hair;
A clock has a face, but no mouth there;
Needles have eyes, but they cannot see;
A fly has a trunk without lock or key;
A timepiece may lose, but cannot win;
A cornfield dimples without a chin;
A hill has no leg, but has a foot;
A wineglass a stem, but not a root;
A watch has hands, but no thumb or finger;
A boot has a tongue, but is no singer;
Rivers run, though they have no feet;
A saw has teeth, but it does not eat;
Ash trees have keys, yet never a lock;
And baby crows, without being a cock.

CHRISTINA ROSSETTI

Thirty white horses upon a red hill,
Now they tramp, now they champ,
Now they stand still.

MOTHER GOOSE

Little Nancy Etticote
In a white petticoat,
With a red nose;
The longer she stands,
The shorter she grows.

MOTHER GOOSE

Runs all day and never walks,
Often murmurs, never talks.
It has a bed but never sleeps,
It has a mouth, but never eats.

MOTHER GOOSE

ANSWERS
the teeth and gums, a candle, a river

Then Samson said to the 30 men,
"Let me tell you a riddle."

JUDGES 14:12

KEEPSAKE MILL

Over the borders, a sin without pardon,
    Breaking the branches and crawling below,
Out through the breach in the wall of the garden,
    Down by the banks of the river, we go.

Here is the mill with the humming of thunder,
    Here is the weir with the wonder of foam,
Here is the sluice with the race running under—
    Marvelous places, though handy to home!

Sounds of the village grow stiller and stiller,
    Stiller the note of the birds on the hill;
Dusty and dim are the eyes of the miller,
    Deaf are his ears with the moil of the mill.

Years may go by, and the wheel in the river
    Wheel as it wheels for us, children, today,
Wheel and keep roaring and foaming for ever
    Long after all of the boys are away.

Home from the Indies and home from the ocean,
    Heroes and soldiers we all shall come home;
Still we shall find the old mill wheel in motion,
    Turning and churning that river to foam.

You with the bean that I gave when we quarreled,
    I with your marble of Saturday last,
Honored and old and all gaily appareled,
    Here we shall meet and remember the past.

ROBERT LOUIS STEVENSON

When life is good, enjoy it.
But when life is hard, remember:
God gives us good times and hard times.
And no one knows what tomorrow will bring.

ECCLESIASTES 7:14

Our greatest glory consists not in never falling,
but in rising every time we fall.

OLIVER GOLDSMITH

THE TEAPOT DRAGON

There's a dragon on our teapot,
　　With a long and crinkly tail,
His claws are like a pincer-bug,
　　His wings are like a sail;

His tongue is always sticking out,
　　And so I used to think
He must be very hungry, or
　　He wanted tea to drink.

But once when Mother wasn't round
　　I dipped my fingers in,
And when I pulled them out I found
　　I'd blistered all the skin.

Now when I see the dragon crawl
　　Around our china pot,
I know he's burned his tongue because
　　The water is so hot.

RUPERT SARGENT HOLLAND

ANIMAL CRACKERS

Animal crackers, and cocoa to drink,
That is the finest of suppers, I think;
When I'm grown up and can have what I please
I think I shall always insist upon these.

What do *you* choose when you're offered a treat?
When Mother says, "What would you like best to eat?"
Is it waffles and syrup, or cinnamon toast?
It's cocoa and animals that *I* love the most!

The kitchen's the coziest place that I know:
The kettle is singing, the stove is aglow,
And there in the twilight, how jolly to see
The cocoa and animals waiting for me.

Daddy and Mother dine later in state,
With Mary to cook for them, Susan to wait;
But they don't have nearly as much fun as I
Who eat in the kitchen with Nurse standing by;
And Daddy once said, he would like to be me
Having cocoa and animals once more for tea!

CHRISTOPHER MORLEY

TO MY NAME-CHILD

Some day soon this rhyming volume, if you learn with proper speed,
Little Louis Sanchez, will be given you to read.
Then shall you discover that your name was printed down
By the English printers, long before, in London town.

In the great and busy city where the East and West are met,
All the little letters did the English printer set;
While you thought of nothing, and were still too young to play,
Foreign people thought of you in places far away.

Ay, and while you slept, a baby, over all the English lands
Other little children took the volume in their hands;
Other children questioned, in their homes across the seas:
Who was little Louis, won't you tell us, mother, please?

Now that you have spelt your lesson, lay it down and go and play,
Seeking shells and seaweed on the sands of Monterey,
Watching all the mighty whalebones, lying buried by the breeze,
Tiny sandy-pipers, and the huge Pacific seas.

And remember in your playing, as the sea fog rolls to you,
Long ere you could read it, how I told you what to do;
And that while you thought of no one, nearly half the world away
Some one thought of Louis on the beach of Monterey!

ROBERT LOUIS STEVENSON

SOME OTHER CHILD

Dear Father, I am very glad
I was the little girl you had!
Suppose some other child had come
To live inside my pleasant home,
To run and climb upon your knee—
Some other child who was not me—
Would you have called her by my name
And thought about her just the same?

MAUDE KEARY

A WAS AN ANGLER

A was an angler,
  Went out in a fog;
Who fish'd all the day,
  And caught only a frog.

B was cook Betty,
  A-baking a pie
With ten or twelve apples
  All piled up on high.

C was a custard
  In a glass dish,
With as much cinnamon
  As you could wish.

D was fat Dick,
  Who did nothing but eat;
He would leave book and play
  For a nice bit of meat.

E was an egg,
  In a basket with more,
Which Peggy will sell
  For a shilling a score.

F was a fox,
  So cunning and sly:
Who looks at the hen-roost—
  I need not say why.

G was a greyhound,
  As fleet as the wind;
In the race or the course
  Left all others behind.

H was a heron,
    Who lived near a pond;
Of gobbling the fishes
    He was wondrously fond.

I was the ice
    On which Billy would skate;
So up went his heels,
    And down went his pate.

J was Joe Jenkins,
    Who played on the fiddle;
He began twenty tunes,
    But left off in the middle.

K was a kitten,
    Who jumped at a cork,
And learned to eat mice
    Without plate, knife, or fork.

L was a lark,
    Who sings us a song,
And wakes us betimes
    Lest we sleep too long.

M was Miss Molly,
    Who turned in her toes,
And hung down her head
    Till her knees touched her nose.

N was a nosegay,
    Sprinkled with dew,
Pulled in the morning
    And presented to you.

O was an owl,
    Who looked wondrously wise;
But he's watching a mouse
    With his large round eyes.

P was a parrot,
    With feathers like gold,
Who talks just as much,
    And no more than he's told.

Q is the Queen
    Who governs the land,
And sits on a throne
    Very lofty and grand.

R is a raven
    Perched on an oak,
Who with a gruff voice
    Cries croak, croak, croak!

S was a stork
    With a very long bill,
Who swallows down fishes
    And frogs to his fill.

T is a trumpeter
    Blowing his horn,
Who tells us the news
    As we rise in the morn.

U is a unicorn,
    Who, as it is said,
Wears an ivory bodkin
    On his forehead.

V is a vulture
    Who eats a great deal,
Devouring a dog
    Or a cat as a meal.

W was a watchman
    Who guarded the street,
Lest robbers or thieves
    The good people should meet.

X was King Xerxes,
    Who, if you don't know,
Reigned over Persia
    A great while ago.

Y is the year
    That is passing away,
And still growing shorter
    Every day.

Z is a zebra,
    Whom you've heard of before;
So here ends my rhyme
    Till I find you some more.

MOTHER GOOSE

I am the Alpha and the Omega,
the First and the Last, the Beginning and the End.
REVELATION 22:13

THE LAND OF COUNTERPANE

When I was sick and lay a-bed,
I had two pillows at my head,
And all my toys beside me lay
To keep me happy all the day.

And sometimes for an hour or so
I watched my leaden soldiers go,
With different uniforms and drills,
Among the bedclothes, through the hills;

And sometimes sent my ships in fleets
All up and down among the sheets;
Or brought my trees and houses out,
And planted cities all about.

I was the giant great and still
That sits upon the pillow-hill,
And sees before him, dale and plain,
The pleasant land of counterpane.

ROBERT LOUIS STEVENSON

To see a World in a Grain of Sand
And a Heaven in a Wild Flower,
Hold Infinity in the palm of your hand
And Eternity in an hour.

WILLIAM BLAKE

I thank the goodness and the grace
Which on my birth have smiled,
And made me, in these Christian days,
A happy Christian child.

JANE TAYLOR

THE NIGHT BEFORE CHRISTMAS

'Twas the night before Christmas, when all through the house
Not a creature was stirring, not even a mouse;
The stockings were hung by the chimney with care,
In hopes that St. Nicholas soon would be there;
The children were nestled all snug in their beds,
While visions of sugarplums danced in their heads;
And Mamma in her kerchief, and I in my cap,
Had just settled our brains for a long winter's nap,
When out on the lawn there arose such a clatter,
I sprang from my bed to see what was the matter.
Away to the window I flew like a flash,
Tore open the shutters and threw up the sash.
The moon, on the breast of the new-fallen snow,
Gave a luster of midday to objects below;
When, what to my wondering eyes should appear,
But a miniature sleigh, and eight tiny reindeer,
With a little old driver, so lively and quick,
I knew in a moment it must be St. Nick.
More rapid than eagles his coursers they came,
And he whistled, and shouted, and called them by name:
"Now, Dasher! now, Dancer! now, Prancer and Vixen!
On, Comet! on, Cupid! on, Donder and Blitzen!
To the top of the porch, to the top of the wall!
Now, dash away, dash away, dash away, all!"

As dry leaves that before the wild hurricane fly,
When they meet with an obstacle, mount to the sky,
So, up to the housetop the coursers they flew,
With the sleigh full of toys—and St. Nicholas, too.
And then in a twinkling I heard on the roof
The prancing and pawing of each little hoof.
As I drew in my head, and was turning around,
Down the chimney St. Nicholas came with a bound.

He was dressed all in fur from his head to his foot,
And his clothes were all tarnished with ashes and soot;
A bundle of toys he had flung on his back,
And he looked like a peddler just opening his pack.

His eyes how they twinkled! his dimples how merry!
His cheeks were like roses, his nose like a cherry;
His droll little mouth was drawn up like a bow,
And the beard on his chin was as white as the snow.
The stump of a pipe he held tight in his teeth,
And the smoke it encircled his head like a wreath;
He had a broad face and a little round belly
That shook, when he laughed, like a bowlful of jelly.

He was chubby and plump—a right jolly old elf;
And I laughed when I saw him, in spite of myself.
A wink of his eye, and a twist of his head,
Soon gave me to know I had nothing to dread.
He spoke not a word, but went straight to his work,
And filled all the stockings; then turned with a jerk,
And laying his finger aside of his nose,
And giving a nod, up the chimney he rose.
He sprang to his sleigh, to his team gave a whistle,
And away they all flew like the down of a thistle;
But I heard him exclaim, ere he drove out of sight,
"Happy Christmas to all, and to all a good night!"

CLEMENT C. MOORE

And a very good Christmas to you all.

ROBERT LOUIS STEVENSON

Today your Savior was born
in David's town.
He is Christ, the Lord.

LUKE 2:11

Blessings
of
Faith

Faith means being sure of the things we hope for.
And faith means knowing that something is real
even if we do not see it.

HEBREWS 11:1

THE LORD'S PRAYER

Our Father in heaven,
we pray that your name will
always be kept holy.
We pray that your kingdom will come.
We pray that what you want will be done,
here on earth as it is in heaven.
Give us the food we need for each day.
Forgive the sins we have done,
just as we have forgiven those
who did wrong to us.
Do not cause us to be tested;
but save us from the Evil One.

MATTHEW 6:9–13

But the truth of His teaching would seem to be this:
In our own person and fortune,
we should be ready to accept and to pardon all;
it is *our* cheek we are to turn,
our coat that we are to give away to the man
who has taken *our* cloak.

ROBERT LOUIS STEVENSON

For God loved the world so much
that he gave his only Son.
God gave his Son so that whoever believes in him
may not be lost, but have eternal life.

JOHN 3:16

I NEVER SAW A MOOR

I never saw a moor,
I never saw the sea;
Yet know I how the heather looks,
And what a wave must be.

I never spoke with God,
Nor visited in heaven;
Yet certain am I of the spot
As if the chart were given.

EMILY DICKINSON

I never weary of great churches.
It is my favorite kind of mountain scenery.

ROBERT LOUIS STEVENSON

Boats sail on the rivers,
And ships sail on the seas;
But clouds that sail across the sky
Are prettier far than these.

There are bridges on the rivers,
As pretty as you please;
But the bow that bridges heaven,
And overtops the trees,
And builds a road from earth to sky,
Is prettier far than these.

CHRISTINA ROSSETTI

Lord, the seas rise up.
The seas raise their voice.
The seas lift up their pounding waves.
The sound of the water is loud.
The ocean waves are powerful.
But the Lord above is much greater.

PSALM 93:3–4

A THOUGHT

It is very nice to think
The world is full of meat and drink,
With little children saying grace
In every Christian kind of place.

ROBERT LOUIS STEVENSON

SONG FOR A LITTLE HOUSE

I'm glad our house is a little house,
Not too tall nor too wide;
I'm glad the hovering butterflies
Feel free to come inside.

Our little house is a friendly house,
It is not shy or vain;
It gossips with the talking trees,
And makes friends with the rain.

And quick leaves cast a shimmer of green
Against our whited walls,
And in the phlox the courteous bees
Are paying duty calls.

CHRISTOPHER MORLEY

There's snow on the fields,
And cold in the cottage,
While I sit in the chimney nook
Supping hot pottage.

My clothes are soft and warm,
Fold upon fold,
But I'm sorry for the poor
Out in the cold.

CHRISTINA ROSSETTI

I will praise you as long as I live. I will lift up my hands in prayer
to your name. I will be content as if I had eaten the best foods.
My lips will sing. My mouth will praise you.

PSALM 63:4–5

LONG, LONG AGO

Winds through the olive trees
   Softly did blow,
Round little Bethlehem
   Long, long ago.

Sheep on the hillside lay
   Whiter than snow;
Shepherds were watching them,
   Long, long ago.

Then from the happy sky,
   Angels bent low,
Singing their songs of joy,
   Long, long ago.

For in a manger bed,
   Cradled we know,
Christ came to Bethlehem,
   Long, long ago.

ANONYMOUS

SONG

Why do the bells of Christmas ring?
Why do little children sing?

Once a lovely shining star,
Seen by shepherds from afar,
Gently moved until its light
Made a manger's cradle bright.

There a darling baby lay,
Pillowed soft upon the hay;
And its mother sung and smiled:
"This is Christ, the holy Child!"

Therefore bells for Christmas ring,
Therefore little children sing.

EUGENE FIELD

The angel said to her, "Don't be afraid, Mary,
because God is pleased with you. Listen! You will become pregnant.
You will give birth to a son, and you will name him Jesus.
He will be great, and people will call him the Son of the Most High.
The Lord God will give him the throne of King David, his ancestor.
He will rule over the people of Jacob forever.
His kingdom will never end."

LUKE 1:30–33

Hope is the thing with feathers
That perches in the soul,
And sings the tune without the words,
And never stops at all,

And sweetest in the gale is heard;
And sore must be the storm
That could abash the little bird
That kept so many warm.

I've heard it in the chillest land,
And on the strangest sea;
Yet, never, in extremity,
It asked a crumb of me.

EMILY DICKINSON

Be like the bird, who
Halting in his flight
On limb too slight
Feels it give way beneath him,
Yet sings
Knowing he hath wings.

VICTOR HUGO

O LITTLE TOWN OF BETHLEHEM

O little town of Bethlehem,

How still we see thee lie.

Above thy deep and dreamless sleep

The silent stars go by;

Yet in thy dark streets shineth

The everlasting Light;

The hopes and fears of all the years

Are met in thee tonight.

PHILLIP BROOKS

I pray that the God who gives hope will fill you with much joy

and peace while you trust in him. Then your hope will overflow

by the power of the Holy Spirit.

ROMANS 15:13

TO MY MOTHER

You too, my mother, read my rhymes

For love of unforgotten times,

And you may chance to hear once more

The little feet along the floor.

ROBERT LOUIS STEVENSON

BABY MINE

Baby mine, over the trees

Baby mine, over the flowers;

Baby mine, over the sunshine;

Baby mine, over the showers.

Baby mine, over the land;

Baby mine, over the water.

Oh, when had a mother before

Such a sweet—such a sweet, little daughter!

KATE GREENAWAY

MY MOTHER

Who dressed my doll in clothes so gay,
And fondly taught me how to play,
And minded all I had to say?
My mother.

Who ran to help me when I fell,
And would some pretty story tell,
Or kiss the place to make it well?
My mother.

Who taught my infant lips to pray,
And love God's holy book and day,
And walk in wisdom's pleasant way?
My mother.

ANN TAYLOR

THE SHEPHERDS HAD AN ANGEL

The Shepherds had an Angel,
  The Wise Men had a star,
But what have I, a little child,
  To guide me home from far,
Where glad stars sing together
  And singing angels are?

Lord Jesus is my Guardian,
  So I can nothing lack:
The lambs lie in His bosom
  Along life's dangerous track:
The willful lambs that go astray
  He bleeding fetches back.

Lord Jesus is my guiding star,
  My beacon-light in heaven:
He leads me step by step along
  The path of life uneven:
He, true light, leads me to that land
  Whose day shall be as seven.

Those Shepherds through the lonely night
  Sat watching by their sheep
Until they saw the heavenly host
  Who neither tire nor sleep
All singing "Glory, glory"
  In festival they keep.

Christ watches me, His little lamb,
  Cares for me day and night,
That I may be His own in heaven:
  So angels clad in white
Shall sing their "Glory, glory"
  For my sake in the height.

The Wise Men left their country
    To journey morn by morn,
With gold and frankincense and myrrh,
    Because the Lord was born:
God sent a star to guide them
    And sent a dream to warn.

My life is like their journey,
    Their star is like God's book;
I must be like those good Wise Men
    With heavenward heart and look:
But shall I give no gifts to God?—
    What precious gifts they took!

Lord, I will give my love to Thee,
    Than gold much costlier,
Sweeter to Thee than frankincense,
    More prized than choicest myrrh:
Lord, make me dearer day by day,
    Day by day holier;

Nearer and dearer day by day;
    Till I my voice unite
And sing my "Glory, glory"
    With angels clad in white;
All "Glory, glory" given to Thee
    Through all the heavenly height.

CHRISTINA ROSSETTI

TO ALISON CUNNINGHAM FROM HER BOY

For the long nights you lay awake
And watched for my unworthy sake:
For your most comfortable hand
That led me through the uneven land:
For all the storybooks you read:
For all the pains you comforted:

* * * * *

From the sick child, now well and old,
Take, nurse, the little book you hold!
And grant it, heaven, that all who read
May find as dear a nurse at need,
And every child who lists my rhyme,
In the bright, fireside, nursery clime,
May hear it in as kind a voice
As made my childish days rejoice!

ROBERT LOUIS STEVENSON

God bless all those that I love.
God bless all those that love me.
God bless all those that love
those that I love, and all those
that love those who love me.

NEW ENGLAND SAMPLER

Day by day, dear Lord, of Thee
Three things I pray:
To see Thee more clearly,
Love Thee more dearly,
Follow Thee more nearly,
Day by day.

RICHARD OF CHICHESTER

THE TWENTY-THIRD PSALM

The Lord is my shepherd.

I have everything I need.

He gives me rest in green pastures.

He leads me to calm water.

He gives me new strength.

For the good of his name,

he leads me on paths that are right.

Even if I walk

through a very dark valley,

I will not be afraid

because you are with me.

Your rod and your walking stick

comfort me.

You prepare a meal for me

in front of my enemies.

You pour oil on my head.

You give me more than I can hold.

Surely your goodness and love will be with me

all my life.

And I will live in the house of the Lord forever.

PSALM 23:1–6

Father, we thank You for the night,
And for the pleasant morning light,
For rest and food and loving care,
And all that makes the day so fair.

Help us to do the things we should,
To be to others kind and good;
In all we do and all we say,
To grow more loving every day.

UNKNOWN

A GOOD BOY

I woke before the morning, I was happy all the day,
I never said an ugly word, but smiled and stuck to play.

And now at last the sun is going down behind the wood,
And I am very happy, for I know that I've been good.

My bed is waiting cool and fresh, with linen smooth and fair,
And I must off to sleepsin-by, and not forget my prayer.

I know that, till tomorrow I shall see the sun arise,
No ugly dream shall fright my mind, no ugly sight my eyes,

But slumber hold me tightly till I waken in the dawn,
And hear the thrushes singing in the lilacs round the lawn.

ROBERT LOUIS STEVENSON

There is no duty we underrate so much
as the duty of being happy.

ROBERT LOUIS STEVENSON

A Robin Redbreast in a Cage
Puts all Heaven in a Rage.

A Skylark wounded in the wing,
A Cherubim does cease to sing.

He who shall hurt the little Wren
Shall never be belov'd by Men.

The wanton Boy that kills the Fly
Shall feel the Spider's enmity.

A truth that's told with bad intent
Beats all the Lies you can invent.

WILLIAM BLAKE

Love all God's creation, the whole and every grain of sand in it.

Love every leaf, every ray of God's light.

Love the animals, love the plants, love everything.

If you love everything, you will perceive the divine mystery in things.

Once you perceive it, you will begin to comprehend it better every day.

And you will come at last to love the whole world

with an all-embracing love.

FYODOR DOSTOYEVSKY

All for You, dear God.

Everything I do,

Or think,

Or say,

The whole day long.

Help me to be good.

UNKNOWN

GRACE FOR A CHILD

Here a little child I stand,
Heaving up my either hand;
Cold as paddocks though they be,
Here I lift them up to Thee,
For a benison to fall
On our meat and on us all.
Amen.

ROBERT HERRICK

God be in my head, and in my understanding;
God be in my eyes, and in my looking;
God be in my mouth, and in my speaking;
God be in my heart, and in my thinking;
God be at my end, and at my departing.

OLD SARUM PRIMER

FROM
HYMNS IN PROSE
FOR CHILDREN

Come, let us praise God, for he is exceeding great;

let us bless God, for he is very good.

He made all things; the sun to rule the day,

the moon to shine by night.

He made the great whale, and the elephant;

and the little worm that crawleth on the ground.

The little birds sing praises to God,

when they warble sweetly in the green shade.

The brooks and rivers praise God,

when they murmur melodiously amongst

the smooth pebbles.

I will praise God with my voice;

for I may praise him,

though I am but a little child.

ANNA LÆTITIA BARBAULD

Love the Lord your God with all your heart, soul and strength.
DEUTERONOMY 6:5

GOD IS THE MAKER OF THE WORLD

For flowers that bloom about our feet,
Father, we thank thee.
For tender grass so fresh, so sweet,
Father, we thank thee.
For song of bird and hum of bee,
For all things fair we hear or see,
Father in heaven, we thank thee.

For blue of stream and blue of sky,
Father, we thank thee.
For pleasant shade of branches high,
Father, we thank thee.
For fragrant air and cooling breeze,
For the beauty of the blooming trees,
Father in heaven, we thank thee.

For this new morning with its light,
Father, we thank thee.
For rest and shelter of the night,
Father, we thank thee.
For health and food, for love and friends,
For everything thy goodness sends,
Father in heaven, we thank thee.

RALPH WALDO EMERSON

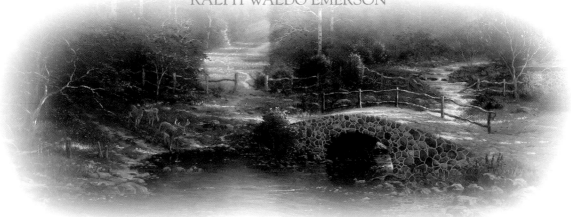

HAPPY THOUGHT

The world is so full of a number of things,
I'm sure we should all be as happy as kings.

ROBERT LOUIS STEVENSON

The year's at the spring,
And day's at the morn;
Morning's at seven;
The hillside's dew-pearled;
The lark's on the wing;
The snail's on the thorn;
God's in His Heaven—
All's right with the world!

ROBERT BROWNING

In the beginning
God created the sky and the earth.

GENESIS 1:1

The Lord is good to me,
and so I thank the Lord.
For giving me the things I need:
the sun, the rain, and the apple seed!
The Lord is good to me.

TRADITIONAL

Thank the Lord because he is good.
His love continues forever.
1 CHRONICLES 16:34

Index of
Paintings
and
Poetry

INDEX OF PAINTINGS

INDEX OF POETRY
BY AUTHORS, FIRST LINES, AND TITLES